Praise for *Why Less is More for WOSPs*

"John Tauer's book is an important addition to the youth sports literature. His description of the research behind intrinsic motivation and other key principles leading to success in sports and life is alone worth the price of the book."

—JIM THOMPSON, FOUNDER AND CEO OF POSITIVE COACHING ALLIANCE

"John Tauer is a highly successful basketball coach as well as a professor of psychology, giving him a unique perspective into how young athletes behave on the court and how their parents behave off it."

—BOB SANSEVERE, *PIONEER PRESS* COLUMNIST AND THE TICKET RADIO TALK SHOW HOST

"This brilliant book, by esteemed scientist, professor, and coach John Tauer, will guide parents back to the essence of sports for their kids—that in athletics, we learn to cooperate and find our strength, passion, and resilience."

—DACHER KELTNER, PH.D.; THOMAS AND RUTH ANN HORNADAY PROFESSOR OF PSYCHOLOGY; DIRECTOR, BERKELEY SOCIAL INTERACTION LABORATORY; FACULTY DIRECTOR, GREATER GOOD SCIENCE CENTER

"As a TV journalist, I've relied on Dr. John Tauer's expertise and research on what motivates us for years. As a dad of two young boys, this is the book I've been waiting for. We all think it's the other parents who are the WOSPs, but John's experience as a player, coach, researcher, and parent might have you wondering if you are the problem. More importantly, he helps us become part of the solution."

—Jason DeRusha, WCCO news anchor,
Twin Cities media personality

"This book is an important contribution to the literature on parenting and coaching young athletes in the twenty-first century. It is well researched, and provides a path for parents to help their children have an enjoyable and successful youth sports experience. It is a great read and I highly recommend it to any parent who truly wants to help a child achieve his or her best."

—John O'Sullivan, founder, Changing the Game Project

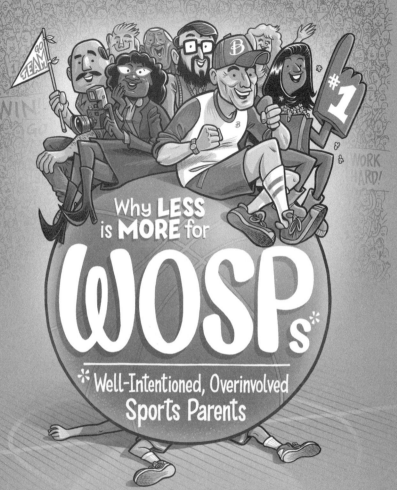

Why LESS is MORE for

WOSPs*

*Well-Intentioned, Overinvolved Sports Parents

How to be the best SPORTS PARENT you can be

by John M. Tauer, Ph.D.

BEAVER'S
POND
PRESS

Illustrated by Kevin Cannon

ISBN 13: 978-1-59298-874-7

Library of Congress Catalog Number: 2015906406

Printed in the United States of America

First Printing: 2015

19   18   17   16   15 5   4   3   2   1

Interior design by James Monroe Design, LLC.

Beaver's Pond Press, Inc.
7108 Ohms Lane, Edina, MN. 55439–2129
(952) 829-8818
www.BeaversPondPress.com

BEAVER'S
POND
PRESS

To order, visit JohnnyTauerBasketball.com

To Mom and Dad, for being wonderful sports parents and providing all the love and support I could have ever asked for. Thank you for never venturing into the hornet's nest of WOSPs.

To Jack and Adam, for inspiring me every day to be a better dad and providing countless days of enjoyment watching you play. May you find your passions in life and remind me gently when I am a WOSP.

Contents

Acknowledgments

This book is the product of several decades of experience with youth sports, which started when I was four years old and continued through my college basketball career. More recently, the last twenty years of my life have focused on motivation research, teaching, coaching, and running camps. Over the past decade, I have also had the chance to watch my sons, Jack and Adam, participate in a variety of youth sports.

Over time, I became painfully aware that parents with the best intentions were doing things in the world of youth sports that ran counter to motivational theory. I saw too many kids to count who became frustrated, burned out, pressured, and overwhelmed by games that started out as fun ways to get physical exercise. That was the impetus for this book. There are countless people to thank, and too little space to adequately do so. Let me start by thanking the tremendous role models I have had in my life, beginning with my parents. They raised me in a way that cultivated intrinsic motivation and encouraged me to chase my dreams. They also attended innumerable sporting events, always in a supportive and enthusiastic manner. For that and so much more, I am eternally indebted to them.

I have been blessed to play for so many outstanding coaches who taught me valuable lessons about athletics. In different ways, they pushed me to be my best and taught me lessons about perseverance, competition, teamwork, and resilience. Steve Fritz, my college coach and now my boss, has been a constant source of motivation, providing friendly reminders to complete this project in a timely manner. Dennis Denning, Randy Muetzel, Len Horyza, Jim Dimick, Dan Brink, Bill McKee, Bob Tschida, and Dick Courtney were influential in my earlier days in sports and, in different ways, each helped inspire me to get into coaching.

On the academic side, my graduate school adviser Judy Harackiewicz was another constant source of motivation, teaching me what it took to study intrinsic motivation and also helping me figure out what it was that I was most intrinsically motivated to do. Research meetings were often delayed by discussions of March Madness and the intersection of our interests in both of those domains provided for many fun discussions of motivation in a variety of settings. John Buri, my undergraduate adviser and now a colleague in the psychology department at the University of St. Thomas, helped a then-clueless sophomore in college enroll in his General Psychology class and the rest is history. Dacher Keltner, Trish Devine, Colleen Moore, Greg Robinson-Riegler, MaryAnne Chalkley, Ann Johnson, and Jean Giebenhain were all wonderful mentors.

I am also indebted to the many colleagues I have coached with the past several years, including Mike Keating, Don Johnson, Jon Hughes, Jay Pivec, Tommy Fritz, Jim Hayes, Alex McCoy, Lonnie Robinson, Paul Weinberg, Jerry Fogerty, and the countless camp coaches who have been a part of so many of these stories. I thank the players I have coached and the students I have taught for their passion, curiosity, and drive to be excellent.

Finally, I am grateful to a number of former University of St. Thomas students (Nikki Arola, Marta Radcliffe, Carolyn Dienhart,

ACKNOWLEDGMENTS

Jeffrey Hilliard, Erin Sprangers, Matt Evans, John Kingsbury, and Greg Morse) for their feedback on earlier versions of this book; to Chancey Anderson for feedback on this entire manuscript; and to my outstanding friends Jon Strausburg, Randy Young, Tom Flood, Matt McDonagh, Shawn Devine, Jim Sticha, Mike Bergan, Glenn Caruso, John Tschida, my coaching colleagues at the University of St. Thomas, and countless others who have engaged in long philosophical discussions about the role of youth sports in our society. The staff at Beaver's Pond Press provided invaluable assistance on all phases of this project: Lily Coyle directed this project; Tom Kerber believed in it; Kevin Cannon provided the illustrations to make WOSPs more vivid; Wendy Weckwerth edited multiple versions of the manuscript; Jay Monroe designed the book; and Alicia Ester managed the details from start to finish. I hope you find this book worthwhile as we all strive to be better parents to our children and coaches to our players as we help them grow and develop and enjoy their experience in youth sports!

1

Welcome to the World of WOSPs

Welcome to the twenty-first century in the wild world of youth sports, where stories of parents screaming and attacking umpires, parents berating coaches, and coaches yelling at and disrespecting players are all in the news far too often. However, a more pervasive and insidious problem in youth sports is the overinvolvement of parents. This overinvolvement, although generally well-intentioned, is what's really ruining sports for our children.

Youth sports have gone crazy. I've been involved in athletics for more than three decades, and never have I been so convinced of this fact as recently when I attended a dinner at my alma mater, Cretin-Derham Hall High School, to honor our legendary baseball coach, Dennis Denning. Coach Denning won six Minnesota State High School League championships in twelve years before moving on to the

University of St. Thomas—where I currently teach and coach. At St. Thomas, he won two National Collegiate Athletic Association (NCAA) Division III national titles and finished second in the nation two other times. Simply put, he is a legend in baseball circles in Minnesota and throughout the Midwest. During his long career, Coach Denning has demonstrated a tremendous commitment to youth sports. For more than thirty years, he has run youth baseball camps. (I attended his camps from ages nine though fourteen.) Coach Denning is a major reason why I chose coaching and working with kids.

That evening as we honored Coach Denning, I bumped into Mike, a longtime acquaintance I hadn't seen in years. We started talking about our kids, our careers, and eventually, youth sports. I mentioned I was writing a book about youth sports, parents, and motivation. Since his kids are a few years older than mine, he had more anecdotes to share. I listened intently as he told me story after story that demonstrated how youth sports were out of control.

My emotions quickly shifted from surprise and curiosity to sadness and shock when Mike told me about a family he knows that wakes their son up at 4:30 a.m. on Saturdays during the summer. After a quick breakfast, they drive an hour to hockey practice, which takes place from 5:30 until 7:30 a.m. Next, they're off to baseball practice from 8:30 to 10:00 a.m. Finally, soccer practice runs from 10:30 a.m. to noon. The US Army has commercials claiming they do more before 9:00 a.m. than most people do all day. This youngster appears to be exercising more before noon than most people do in a week.

You might be thinking this kid must be on the road to athletic stardom, so he needs to do all that to maintain a spot on his high school varsity teams. You might assume he's well on his way to a college scholarship. Imagine my reaction when I heard that we'd have to wait several years to see whether or not this boy will play in high school, much less college. The reason? He's only eight years old! In this moment—after three decades of involvement with youth sports, first as a participant and then as a coach—I became aware of just how severely I had underestimated the bizarre world of youth sports.

Until that conversation with Mike, I had been writing this book under the assumption that I had a pretty good handle on the culture of youth sports given my twenty years of experience in related fields. I had coached college basketball for well over a decade, researched motivation in students and athletes as a college professor, directed my own youth basketball camps for twenty years (working with thousands of kids), and raised two young children of my own. However, not even this experience adequately prepared me for the extremes of parental behavior when it came to this subject.

I had dozens of tales from camp, coaching, and the classroom that illustrated good and bad examples of motivation on and off the athletic courts and fields. After that conversation with Mike, though, I conducted more focused research on the topic of youth sports and parenting. In that process, I encountered an increasingly greater number of parents who had stories similar to those Mike shared about the perils of youth sports. Unfortunately, I heard relatively few stories that highlighted the resilience of a youngster who outworked everyone else or an underdog team that overcame staggering odds. It surprised me that these parents' stories about youth sports typically didn't involve kids at all. This was a paradox. How could most of the stories I was being told be focused on parents, rather than the kids playing the games? Most stories centered on how parents were making youth sports unpleasant, even miserable, for their children, coaches, umpires, league commissioners, and themselves.

I've been amazed at how the topic of youth sports touches a nerve in so many parents. For years, when people asked me what I did, I excitedly described my research on intrinsic motivation, a unique type of motivation that involves the desire to take part in an activity for its own sake, rather than for money or rewards. Others seemed less enthusiastic than I was about theoretical models tested by experimental studies that identified mediating variables of intrinsic motivation. Most people nodded their heads and smiled politely, and then changed the subject by asking me if I was psychoanalyzing them. However, these lukewarm responses to my description of my research changed when I started describing my research on youth sports. Invariably, parents' eyes would light up (in stark contrast to the polite smiles they'd displayed when I was boring them with the minutiae of my research on intrinsic motivation), and they would proceed to regale me with story after story of outlandish parental behavior at youth sporting events.

Psychologists often struggle to collect sufficient data for our research projects, but it quickly became apparent that accumulating anecdotes and data would not be the challenge in this project. In most cases, these parents' stories weren't about physical violence, or even verbal aggression. Most centered on how children's and parents' lives are consumed by youth sports. I was struck by how eager parents were to discuss these stories and how willing they were to be candid about their own struggles in these areas. I was intrigued by their motivation to become so involved in their children's athletic endeavors and how much excitement they had for this book. Parents repeatedly brought up their frustrations with the time, money, and energy expended on youth sports. Before I go any further, I want to acknowledge three points.

First, I believe the vast majority of parents with children in sports are well-intentioned, but overinvolved. Throughout this book, I will refer to these parents as WOSPs—Well-intentioned, Overinvolved Sports Parents. My hunch is that you're reading this book because you care deeply about the welfare of children. They are literally and figuratively our future. However, I believe an excessive amount of these good intentions, specifically in the domain of youth sports, can prove damaging to our children's development. Here's my conclusion: WOSPs can do more good for their children by doing less.

Second, I have two sons: Jack is twelve years old and Adam is ten. Given that Jack was on a T-ball team at age two, a soccer team at age three, and attended my basketball camp at age four, I'm not here to point fingers at other parents who encourage their children to participate in sports at a young age. Moreover, I'm not proposing that we eliminate youth sports. Youth sports have the potential to provide numerous benefits to our kids, including teamwork, competitiveness, discipline, perseverance, and dedication. However, youth sports have become so pervasive in our culture that we have come to assume that these benefits are their inevitable by-product, but we rarely stop to examine whether or not these benefits are actually being realized by our children. We don't often examine carefully at what age and how much youth sports ought to be integrated into our children's lives.

Third, according to social psychologists, humans have two basic social needs: the need to feel good and the need to be good. WOSPs typically possess both of these goals for their children. WOSPs want their kids to feel good (have high self-esteem) and to be good (perform at a high level). Although there's nothing inherently wrong with either of these goals (there's actually quite a bit right about them), an excessive emphasis on self-esteem (the need to feel good) or winning (the need to be good) can create serious problems for children and parents alike.

I'm convinced that parents mean well. I'm also convinced that youth sports can benefit children. At the same time, I believe that as they operate now, youth sports are in a state of hyperorganized disarray. Fortunately, we know enough about optimal conditions for motivation to make changes in the ways our children participate in sports. When it comes to youth sports and the lessons children are learning, there's work to do but much of it starts with us as parents, not with our children. The irony is that at no time in our country's history have parents invested so much time, energy, and money attempting to raise their kids well. Whether it be with private tutors, personal trainers, or participation on traveling teams, parents are going to extreme lengths to provide opportunities for their children. However, it appears that many of these attempts aren't benefiting children in the short- and long-term ways we might hope.

The central premise of this book is that when it comes to youth sports, parents' good intentions often go overboard. Based on research in sports and social psychology, I will present factors that help us understand (1) why parental overinvolvement occurs, (2) what effects parental overinvolvement have on children, (3) how overinvolvement affects the parents who have gone overboard, and (4) what measures we can implement to restore sanity in youth sports.

Most parents encourage their children to participate in sports. There are a multitude of reasons for this, including the social, physical, cognitive, and psychological benefits. But you don't have to be a sports fanatic (or a social psychologist who studies motivation) to come across a plethora of stories that highlight how problematic youth sports have become. Among those stories, we can identify a wide range of good, bad, and ugly effects among well-intentioned parents. In honor of the backwards nature of youth sports today, we'll examine these good, bad, and ugly effects of youth sports in reverse order.

The Ugly

Let's start with the ugly scenes from youth sports—stories that all too frequently are found on the front page or as the lead story on the evening news. Consider horrific headlines such as "Dad Threatened Son's Coach with Gun." Sadly, this is an actual headline. Wayne Derkotch of Philadelphia pulled out a gun after becoming enraged because he felt his son wasn't receiving sufficient playing time on his youth football team. It's difficult to pinpoint the most frightening part of this story. A man pulling a .357 Magnum at a football game? A man pulling a gun because he believes his son hasn't had enough playing time? Five- and six-year-olds playing football in a peewee league? While all of these are troubling, the most disturbing may be the coach's comment after the game, that he sees parents like that all the time. Have youth sports become so twisted that a man wielding a gun at a football game played by five- and six-year-olds is nothing more than what the coach deemed an "unfortunate situation"?[1]

While I believe ugly cases remain the exceptions, it is becoming more common for coaches to receive threats like the one received by Noe Ambriz, a youth baseball coach in Saint Paul, Minnesota. Wade Campbell's son wasn't playing as much as his father would have liked. Campbell responded by unleashing a profanity-laced tirade, complete with racial slurs, toward Coach Ambriz, and in front of the twelve-year-olds on the Little League baseball team. Campbell was quickly escorted off the grounds. Apparently he wasn't satisfied that he'd gotten his point across, because he proceeded to sit outside Ambriz's home for several hours the next day, staring at the coach. In a subsequent

---

1.   Lloyd Vries, "Cops: Dad Threatened Son's Coach with Gun," cbsnews.com, October 24, 2006, http://www.cbsnews.com/news/cops-dad-threatened-sons-coach-with-gun/.

phone call, Campbell allegedly threatened Ambriz's life. It's hard to fathom that these threats stemmed from a dispute over playing time in a Little League game.

Sometimes parental aggression is directed not at coaches, but at umpires and referees. Take, for example, the coach of a peewee football team in Nebraska who punched a sixteen-year-old referee, or the parent in Ohio who threatened a referee with a gun. Recently, a colleague of mine was at his son's youth football game. The boy's coach played college football for a national powerhouse and coached the boys with an intensity usually reserved for that level. As the coach was yelling and screaming at his players and the referees during the game, some parents shouted out from the stands that the coach should calm down. Within seconds, the coach had sprinted into the stands and was involved in a confrontation with the parents that led to the coach being suspended.

Other times, the violence can more directly impact young athletes. A father coaching youth football in California was upset about an illegal tackle and proceeded to sprint onto the field and viciously tackle the offending player. This incident was caught on camera and quickly generated hundreds of thousands of hits on YouTube. A father in Las Vegas was unhappy that his son was being teased after practice, so he filled his son's water bottle with syrup of ipecac. His goal? Induce vomiting on the part of the bully. His plan went awry when eight members of the team drank from the water bottle, leading to violent vomiting, and a mass exodus from football practice to the hospital. Parental behavior doesn't get much more sickening than this (pun intended).

Sometimes the consequences of parents' behavior are even more dire than an emergency room visit. Consider the story out of Reading, Massachusetts, where one father beat another father to death. The cause of the fight? Alleged rough play that was being allowed in a hockey game. Talk about an eye for an eye—these parents are engaging in what seems to be a life for a limb.

Although twisted and clearly misguided in their actions, my hunch is that all of these offending parents began with wanting what was best for their children. At some point, the parents crossed a line and were unable control their emotions. As we read these types of stories, it's easy to conclude that a sizable contingent of parents are dangers to other coaches, parents, and children. But are these events as common as we might think? What does the research tell us about the frequency of parents behaving badly?

A 2001 survey by Survey USA asked five hundred parents a series of questions about parental behavior at youth sporting events. Among their findings:

- 55 percent had witnessed verbally abusive parents at youth sporting events.

- 21 percent had seen a physical altercation between other parents at youth sporting events.

- 73 percent felt parents who are either verbally or physically abusive during games should be disallowed at subsequent games (22 percent would allow these parents to remain in the stands, while 5 percent weren't sure what to do).[2]

At first glance, these survey results appear to indicate that verbal and physical aggression are relatively normal occurrences, consistent with Coach Wilson's observation of the father with the .357 Magnum.

---

2. "Recommendations for Communities Developed through the National Summit on Raising Community Standards in Children's Sports," http://www.nays.org/CMSContent/File/nays_community_recommendations.pdf.

However, a closer inspection of the data indicates these incidents may still be quite rare. For example, the 21 percent of people who have seen an altercation at a youth sporting event may represent parents who have been to hundreds of games and seen one violent incident committed by one parent. Furthermore, large groups of parents may have seen the same single, isolated event. For example, at a large soccer tournament, if one parent gets into an altercation with a referee, and hundreds of parents either saw this up close or from a distance, all of those parents would now forever respond "yes" to any question asking if they've ever witnessed physical aggression at a youth sporting event. Yet the sum total of violent incidents they had seen would have only been one. Taken a step further, imagine a clip on YouTube of parents fighting at a football game. How would a parent who has viewed that clip respond to the questions above? In sum, these data tell us what people have seen at least one time, but they don't tell us about the overall frequency of these events.

Our perception of violence at youth sporting events may be distorted by the media coverage of these events. Today, if a parent attacks a coach, it's likely to receive attention on most major websites (e.g., cnn.com, msnbc.com). Years ago, word of similar incidents would have traveled much more slowly; rarely would video footage of the event be available; and there were fewer outlets for publicity. Violent episodes that may have remained local stories in years past can now be viewed around the world within days.

This attention to the ugly aspects of youth sports can lead to an exaggerated perception of violence at youth sporting events. This kind of availability heuristic occurs whenever we overestimate the likelihood of an event based on how easily it comes to mind. For example, people believe they are much more likely to die on an airplane than in a car, even though the statistics provide overwhelming evidence that driving is more dangerous than flying. Vivid images of airplane crashes get etched in our memory, whereas far more frequent deaths due to car accidents, cancer, or heart disease are less publicized and less readily available scenarios to our imaginations. In the same way, parental rage at youth sporting events receives enormous media coverage, quickly leading us to exaggerate its frequency.

Although one violent act at a youth sporting event is one too many, our tendency to focus on these relatively rare occurrences of parental rage may obscure a far more pervasive problem with parenting. This issue is more chronic and insidious, and involves the well-intentioned, overinvolved sports parents (WOSPs) who stress out both parent and child in the process, undermining many of the valuable benefits we hope our children derive from athletics. This more common occurrence of parental overinvolvement includes the behavior of millions of WOSPs buzzing around the world of youth sports.

The Bad

Everyone can agree that the violent youth-sports anecdotes described earlier are egregious acts. Even the parents involved in these incidents would be hard-pressed to justify their behavior. These events are clearly a problem, yet they occur far less frequently than the media might have us believe. One way to think of parental behavior is along a continuum, ranging from underinvolved to overinvolved. Statistically speaking, most parents reside in the middle of this continuum.

Research indicates there are clear drawbacks for children of underinvolved parents. Each year, I ride along with a good friend of mine who works in the Gang Unit of the Saint Paul Police Department.

Most of the juveniles he arrests have little or no parental supervision or involvement. In some instances, their parents may be incarcerated. In other cases, they're unavailable for contact about the arrest. These are clear examples of how parents who are uninvolved hinder their children. In fact, there is a large body of evidence that indicates uninvolved parents are little help to their children.

Most well-intentioned parents strive to be involved in their children's lives. Ironically, their earnest efforts to help their children are the origin of many extreme examples of parental rage. A host of factors conspire to lead many parents to err on the side of overinvolvement. We live in a culture of extremes. If being involved is good, we assume more involvement is better. If Billy played on one traveling team last year, would two be better this year? If he plays on two traveling teams this year, would three teams be better for him next summer? If Maria played forty softball games last summer, wouldn't fifty games this summer be better for her? Like most things in life, we assume more is better and forget that too much of a good thing can boomerang into a bad thing.

Becoming overinvolved in youth sports is a slippery slope that can lead parents and children into a cycle of unhealthy behavior. Overinvolvement isn't limited to youth sports, though. The term "helicopter parents" has become a description for parents of college students who remain intimately close to their sons and daughters during their time in college. It's common for some students to talk to their parents multiple times each day. These conversations may range from updating mom and dad on an exam, a relationship, or simply that day's mediocre cafeteria offerings. These frequent interactions represent a relatively recent and marked departure from the days when college was seen as the last rite of passage into adulthood.

Students went away to college and were quite literally on their own. Due in large part to technological advances such as the cell phone, which University of Georgia professor Richard Mullendore aptly calls "the world's longest umbilical cord," college students can now rely on their parents for everything from paying tuition to confronting a teacher or coach about an unpleasant exam or practice. More parents than ever before contact teachers, professors, and coaches.

Of course, parents don't magically transform into helicopter parents when a child turns eighteen and goes to college. Their helicopter rotor has typically been running on high for more than a decade. They're well-polished machines that have withstood the test of time—due in part to constant social pressure from other parents and the media to provide a pain-free existence for their children. Many times, helicopter parents have honed their well-intentioned hovering during years of youth sports.

It is easy to imagine how extreme levels of parental involvement can cause a range of problems for children. It's all too common that I hear stories of burnout, frustration, parents yelling, pressure, and children having no fun—all of which highlight how parental overinvolvement can lead to problems for young athletes.

Whether it's academic or athletic burnout, diminished motivation, inability to cope with new situations, increased anxiety due to performance pressure, fear of failure, difficulty negotiating conflict, or a lack of creativity and independence, the overinvolved parent ironically brings about the opposite effects that he or she intended.

I will never forget the moments when my two sons were born. Each time, it was as if my world changed, with an intense focus on Jack and Adam as the centers of my world. While this sounds selfless, it can also become dangerous if this were to remain the case throughout their childhood years. My belief that my two sons are the most special children in the world, and your parallel belief (about your own child, not mine) are the result evolutionary adaptation. It leads parents to invest inordinate amounts of time and energy into successfully raising our children in an effort to pass on the family genes. This belief that one's own child is extra special also leads parents to expect extra-special things of their children. These goals for children can take many forms: being an excellent human being, an outstanding student, and a star athlete. For many WOSPs, the athletic part of this vision carries more weight than it ought to carry.

The Good: The Story of the All-American Athlete

With all these potential unintended negative consequences, why then do we encourage youth to participate in sports? Most of us hope our children will learn invaluable life lessons and skills—including teamwork, goal setting, discipline, determination, an ability to handle success and failure with grace and dignity, and an appreciation for hard work as a means to achieving a goal.

Good examples of youth sports and success abound: kids who overcame long odds, teams that stuck together during turmoil, kids who learned the value of a strong work ethic and perseverance, comebacks, underdog stories, and life lessons learned on the court. Most parents wouldn't be opposed to their child growing up to be an All-American athlete, but would hope the achievement occurs in a healthy environment not utterly dominated by sports.

The Good of Sports

On a snowy Minnesota evening in December 2000, I observed the single-most impressive individual performance in a high school basketball game I had ever witnessed. Playing for Cretin-Derham Hall against rival, top-ranked Highland Park High School, an unassuming six-foot-four senior forward scored thirty-one points and had eleven rebounds and eleven assists. He did this without missing a single shot, going ten for ten from the field (with one three-point basket) and ten for ten from the free-throw line. It was as close to a perfectly played game of basketball as I've ever seen—and I've seen thousands of games. This player had just dismantled one of the top teams in the state. He'd also won an individual match-up with Mo Hargrow, Highland Park's nationally recruited star who would go on to start at the University of Minnesota. What made this performance even more remarkable was that basketball wasn't this player's best sport, or even his second best. Basketball was a distant third for this eighteen-year-old All-American, behind both football and baseball.

Joe Mauer had flown home that afternoon for the basketball game versus Highland Park, having just completed his official football recruiting visit to the University of Arizona. An Arizona football coach had flown back with him to Minnesota. The coach attended the basketball game, and afterward said he was willing to stay in Minnesota until Mauer decided to return to Arizona with him. He sounded as if he were only half joking. The University of Minnesota basketball coach at the time, Dan Monson, was at the game, and someone asked him if he thought he might be recruiting the wrong number eleven (Hargrow and Mauer, who grew up playing together at the same rec center, both wore number eleven on their jerseys). Monson could only muster a nervous laugh.

In football, Mauer was an All-American quarterback who had led his team to a state championship as a junior, the first state football title in school history. He was the highest-rated quarterback in the country, and Gatorade, *Parade* magazine, and *USA Today* all named him their National High School Football Player of the Year.

Amazingly, Mauer was even better in baseball. He batted over .600, while striking out only once in his high school career. He shattered nearly every record at Cretin-Derham Hall, a storied program that had won nine of the previous eighteen state titles, with numerous players selected in the Major League Baseball (MLB) draft. Mauer was also named *USA Today* National Player of the Year in baseball. He is the only athlete in history to have been honored as the *USA Today* National Player of the Year in football and baseball.

During his senior year of high school, Mauer led his football team to a second-place finish at the state tournament (after winning the title the year before), his basketball team to a third-place finish, and his baseball team to the state championship. He signed with Florida State University to play quarterback. The Minnesota Twins held the number-one pick in that year's MLB draft. The entire state of Minnesota buzzed for weeks about whether the Twins would use the pick to select Mauer. The Twins debated the merits of several other players besides Mauer, including Mark Prior of the University of Southern California, who was projected to be the best pitching prospect since Roger Clemens. Ultimately, Minnesota selected Mauer with the first pick. National Player of the Year in two sports, state champion in two sports, All-State in three sports, recruited by every university in the country, and now the top pick in the MLB draft. Sounds like the profile of a childhood sports prodigy. Indeed, Mauer's talents were evident at a very young age. What was the source of his talent? And what role did his parents play in his development?

What makes Joe Mauer's story so interesting lies more in what his parents didn't do as opposed to what they did, and in who Joe Mauer isn't, as much as who he is. Joe's parents, Jake and Teresa, weren't over-involved. They didn't coddle Joe because of his ability, nor did they spend extraordinary amounts of money to help Joe specialize in one sport at a very young age. Not every child will grow up to be a star athlete like Joe Mauer, but we could all take a lesson from the Mauers about how to parent in a manner that uses sports to help teach life lessons in discipline, loyalty, teamwork, commitment, respect, and motivation. The Mauers are successful parents not because Joe turned into an MVP and three-time American League batting champion, but because he and his brothers Jake and Billy are excellent people with strong values. So many of the positive outcomes of youth sports are embodied in the Mauer family, and we'll return to their story.

Throughout this book, I use notable athletes and their parents as examples to illustrate psychological concepts and theories relevant to youth sports, parenting, and motivation. In Chapter 2, we take a brief step back in time to understand the origin of youth sports and how we got to this point. To determine whether youth sports are succeeding or failing, and why the bad and the ugly seem to outweigh the good, we must identify the original goals of youth sports.

Words of Wisdom for WOSPs

1. Be involved in your child's life, but not too involved.
    Finding a balance of involvement is an ongoing process.
    Recognize that your love for your children and your desire

for them to live happy and productive lives may lead you to err on the side of overinvolvement.

2. Staying out of fights at youth sports is not a badge of honor. The real challenge for most parents is staying out of our children's way in less public ways—and allowing our kids to enjoy sports and their childhood!

3. Remember the goals of youth sports. What are your goals? What are your child's goals? Put yourself in your child's shoes. Are they enjoying their experiences? Are they learning valuable lessons? Do they have some choice about their activities? Make time to regularly talk to them about their goals and their experiences in sports.

2

A History of Youth Sports from a Social-Psychological Perspective

With childhood obesity reaching epidemic levels, former US Surgeon General C. Everett Koop recently wrote an article for cnn.com with the simple headline "Kick the Kids Outside to Play," encouraging parents to kick kids out of the house (temporarily, of course) so they'll play games outside with other kids in their neighborhoods. It's a sad day when kids have to be forced to *play*.[3]

One of my close friends, Tom, grew up in a family with thirteen kids and little money to spare. Tom and his siblings tell stories that

---

3.   Dr. C. Everett Koop, "Dr. Koop: Kick the kids outside to play," July 23, 2010, http://www.cnn.com/2010/OPINION/07/23/koop.kids.street.games/.

highlight making do with next to nothing when it came to meals, hand-me-down clothing, running water, and sports. The family didn't have the money for a basketball hoop, so Tom and his brothers took a twenty-inch bicycle wheel, pulled out the spokes, and nailed it to a tree. (That story has been an excuse for me to joke with Tom that a regulation rim is only eighteen inches in diameter, so their oversized, makeshift version explains his dismal shooting accuracy.) For the rest of the summer, kids from their neighborhood spent countless hours shooting baskets at that bicycle wheel. The creativity and resourcefulness demonstrated by Tom and his siblings are examples of what kids can learn from sports. Unfortunately, youth sports have become so organized and parent-driven over the past couple decades, children aren't allowed to learn some of the most valuable lessons sports have to offer.

Gone Are the Days of Pickup Games

I was in a gymnasium with forty kids who were attending a week-long camp. The kids were broken up into ten teams of four to play half-court games. We had five baskets and four coaches (referees) in the gym. Given the shortage of a referee for one of the baskets, and our goal of keeping the kids active and working hard, I presented campers with two options.

Option one: We'd play five rounds of games, with each team playing games in four of the five rounds. Each team would sit out one round. All of the games would be refereed.

Option two: We'd play five rounds of games, with each team playing games in all five rounds. Four of the five games would be refereed.

Each team would play one game in which they refereed their own game, calling their own fouls and keeping track of the score. Assuming the campers enjoyed playing basketball, I thought the second option would be the easy winner.

To my amazement, thirty-two of forty campers (80 percent of them) chose the first option. Essentially, the campers were saying: "If given the choice of playing without a referee or not playing at all, we'd prefer not to play." This was one of the most shocking experiences of my coaching career. Eighty percent of children who chose to attend basketball camp during their summer break preferred to sit and do nothing than to play a game without a referee!

My mind was racing with negative stereotypes of kids today, but before I jumped to conclusions, I decided to give the campers the benefit of the doubt. It was entirely possible that the reason they would have preferred to sit out was because they thought they would be too tired to play in five consecutive games. Of course, each game was only five minutes in length, and there was a two-minute break in between games, so playing five consecutive rounds wouldn't take their bodies to exhaustion. I secretly hoped that fear of fatigue would be the answer. I proceeded to ask the group of campers why they chose not to play all five rounds. Hands shot up throughout the gym.

"Because we'll disagree about foul calls!" responded one child. Other kids nodded in agreement.

"We'll lose track of the score," said another, as several more nodded in agreement.

"We won't know how much time is left in the game."

"We'll fight about who wins."

"We'll forget to substitute players in and out of the game."

"We'll argue about the rules."

Six kids, six different responses, and not one mentioned fatigue.

Instead, every one of the responses focused on the perceived inability of the campers to manage a game and get along with one another in the absence of adult supervision. I have shared this story with numerous parents and they have been as astounded by the results as I was. Kids chose sitting out over playing if a referee couldn't be involved. What does this tell us about children's reliance on structure? To what extent have formal sports (and WOSPs) created this problematic dependence in our children? What does this tell us about children's ability to negotiate conflict, enforce rules, and keep track of basic items such as the score of a game?

Many of my fondest childhood memories involve pickup baseball games at local parks with my friends from grade school. Typically, I'd call a few of my friends to see if they wanted to meet at the park. Almost invariably, the answer would be yes, and they'd proceed to call others in a literal game of telephone. Within the hour, ten to fifteen of us would meet up at the park, pick two captains, and select teams. Of course, this could lead to hurt feelings, since the poorer players would be chosen later than the more talented ones. Additionally, one team might have eight players while the other only had seven. Or, we might only have ten players, so we'd play five-on-five baseball, using only half the field. Other times, we played on my friend Matt's boulevard. The median in the middle of the street was the pitcher's mound and the house across the street had a huge hill that simulated Fenway Park's Green Monster. We'd play two-on-two or three-on-three, depending on how many people were available. Other days, we'd go to the park and play pickup basketball. Those games ranged from one-on-one to five-on-five, or even just two friends coming up with different shooting competitions.

Regardless of the game, calls were occasionally argued, and there were periodic disputes about either the score or a rules interpretation.

Sometimes tempers flared and pushing or shoving ensued. Somehow, though, despite our occasional controversies, and without the assistance of parents, coaches, umpires, or referees, we always seemed to meet up at the park again the next day. Even on days when a couple of us got in a skirmish, the fights could be measured in minutes while the games lasted for hours.

Fast-forward twenty-five years. There are more parks and recreation centers today than ever before—with better equipment and more supervision. However, when I visit one of our local parks these days, I typically see one of two scenes. Scene one: On a walk to the park, I see other parents with young children who are playing on the slides and swings, but not a soul is on the basketball courts or the baseball, softball, or soccer fields. Scene two: On a walk to the park, I pass by two girls' soccer teams playing each other. Adjacent to this is a T-ball game for young children, which is next to a baseball game for adolescent boys, and all of these aren't far from a tennis camp for high school athletes.

In the first scenario, we see an apparent apathy for athletics without supervision or formal structure. In the absence of organized sports, fields and courts go virtually unused. In the second scenario, we see what appears to be extreme interest in structured sports, with a specific coach instructing each team, referees making calls, and parents watching from the sidelines. Each of these scenarios is a dramatic departure from what one would have seen several decades ago when it was much more common for a group of children to meet up at the park, pick their own teams, call their own balls and strikes, keep track of the score by themselves, and play and run and argue and laugh to their hearts' content. Today, it's rare to see children at a park without their parents, and without some structured activity. In fact, children appear to have become so accustomed to structured activities that they have trouble functioning without them.

I understand and even advocate for organized and structured sports activities. I have run my own summer basketball camps (Johnny Tauer's Championship Basketball Camp) for the past eighteen years. During that time, I've worked with thousands of young athletes. After teaching psychology and coaching basketball at the college level during the academic year, it's a nice change of pace to work with younger children during the summer months. Kids have a different level of curiosity, and invariably their excitement becomes contagious for me and all of my coaches. My sense is that the vast majority of kids enjoy camp because they enjoy basketball, they get to spend time with old and new friends, and they get to work with enthusiastic and knowledgeable coaches who challenge them and keep them active. We never want campers sitting out for very long; we want them to understand what it takes to learn and improve, and we want them to see that working hard and having fun can happen at the same time. In sum, we want the campers to experience the plethora of benefits youth sports can offer. But the structured atmosphere of a camp shouldn't be the only place kids access the fun and lessons to be found in sports.

The anecdotes I've just shared highlight a decreasing ability—perhaps even a decreasing desire—among children to develop some of the very social skills that athletics are intended to develop. Children today aren't biologically different than kids fifty years ago, so what's changed? To make an educated theory, we must first explore how sports became so prevalent in our culture, and how they've evolved.

A Brief History of Sports

Knowledge of the benefits of physical fitness and sports is nothing new. For centuries, people have understood the connection between a healthy body and a healthy mind. As far back as 3000 to 1500 BCE, the Egyptians were engaged in a variety of games.[4] Physical activity was also a hallmark of Greek society; the first Olympic competition took place in 776 BCE.[5] Benefits attributed to exercise and sport include physical, social, and cognitive development; sportspersonship; setting goals; learning how to win gracefully; learning from feedback and/or failure; resiliency; discipline; competitiveness; teamwork; and career preparation. In sum, there are numerous potential benefits of athletic participation.

Of course, there are potential downsides to an extreme emphasis on athletic endeavors. An overemphasis on winning, fame, and glory can have detrimental effects at both the individual and societal level. If athletic success becomes the ultimate goal for individuals, many of the potential benefits, e.g., teamwork and unselfishness, may not be realized. On a societal level, an extreme focus on sports may lead a culture to overvalue sports. When one considers the attention and resources given to sports compared to community events or societal problems, it's clear that sports can be viewed as an end in itself, as opposed to a training ground to develop skills that will serve one well in many areas of life. According to sports psychologists Arnold LeUnes and Jack R. Nation:

---

4. E.F. Ziegler (Ed.) *A History of Sport and Physical Education to 1900.* (Champaign, IL: Stipes, 1973).

5. Arnold LeUnes and Jack R. Nation, *Sports Psychology*, 3rd ed. (Pacific Grove, CA: Wadsworth, 2002), 27.

An expansion of the concept of democratic government
gave citizens a greater voice in matters related to their own
welfare. Tremendous emphasis was placed on the enhance-
ment of individual freedoms. Physical education became
a means of self-enhancement and self-expression, and the
utilitarian aspects of physical and military preparedness
were neglected. The needs and wishes of individuals took
precedence over the welfare of the city-state. Professionalism
began to change the nature of athletic events, thus encouraging spectatorship rather than participation. The masses
looked to athletic events for amusement. (30)

What time period do you think they were describing in the passage above? Although it could have been written to describe a time a
few decades ago, it also provides an apt depiction of contemporary
American sports. Amazingly, the passage described the Greek empire
around 400 BCE, after they defeated the Persian Army!

Thousands of years ago, Plato and other Greek philosophers
lamented that the values sports were supposed to be teaching were
being overlooked. Since the 1700s, schools in the United States
have promoted physical education—following Benjamin Franklin's
encouragement to promote physical activity among their students.
Some historians argue that the post-Civil War period was critical in
the development of youth sports. Due to an increase in disciplinary
problems with urban youths, youth sports were seen as a useful tool
through which to instill the discipline, character, and values present in previous generations.[6] In 1956, President Eisenhower created

6.   President's Council on Fitness, Sports & Nutrition, "Our History," http://www.
fitness.gov/about-pcfsn/our-history/.

the Presidential Council on Physical Fitness and Sports (called the President's Council on Fitness, Sports and Nutrition since 2010) that laid out standards for the physical fitness of elementary school students. Over the centuries, the emphasis on physical activity has waxed and waned, in part due to the surrounding economic and social conditions.

Today, many children are still tested on pull-ups, sit-ups, and running. However, the pendulum appears to have swung back, with schools emphasizing standardized test scores, but rarely requiring daily physical education. As we look at the twenty-first century, we see a level of organization in youth sports that would make the Greek military proud. While schools have become comparatively removed from physical education, youth sports have exploded. Whether it is Little League Baseball, Pop Warner football, Amateur Athletic Union (AAU) basketball, or club soccer, kids today have unparalleled opportunities to engage in competitive sports. Researchers estimate that tens of millions of American children are involved in competitive youth sports in any given year, a number that has risen consistently over the past twenty years.[7] Competitive youth sports, which began as an outlet for children to develop physical strength, fitness, character, and values, has become a training ground for children to hone their skills and compete year-round in pursuit of championships, trophies, college scholarships, and multimillion-dollar professional contracts.

---

7.   Bruce Kelley and Carl Carchia, *ESPN The Magazine*, July 10, 2013, http://espn.go.com/espn/story/_/id/9469252/hidden-demographics-youth-sports-espn-magazine.

Goals of Sports

Not surprisingly, when children and parents are asked about the benefits of youth sports, they typically don't begin by listing wealth, fame, and prestige as their goals. In fact, in numerous studies exploring the motives for participation in youth sports, a clear and consistent answer emerges from the question, "What is the primary reason you participate in sports?" The response: to have fun.[8] *Fun* is an amalgam of numerous variables that help produce an enjoyable experience. Fun may come from making friends, learning, improving, working hard, winning, and simply playing. Other factors that lead to participation in sports include following role models, competition, social factors, extrinsic rewards, and prestige. However, it seems unlikely that fun can be the sole factor that explains kids spending their entire childhoods hitting tennis balls, shooting basketballs, or throwing baseballs at the expense of a balanced life.

Why Has the Culture of Youth Sports Changed?

Evolutionary forces don't exert striking changes in populations over several years, much less several generations. Given that children today are biologically similar to children several decades ago, and the same is true of parents, what factors help explain this radical shift away from the original goals of youth sports? There are several explanations, many of which are interrelated. I will return to many of these topics throughout the book, but I want to set the stage for an

---

8.   Robert Weinberg and Daniel Gould. *Foundations of Sport and Exercise Psychology.* (Human Kinetics: Champign, IL, 2015).

understanding of cultural change in youth sports due to money, fear, conformity, parental pressure, and traveling teams.

Money: If It Don't Make Dollars, Then It Don't Make Sense

The average salaries of professional athletes today dwarf those of their predecessors. Pro players thirty or fifty years ago typically still held other jobs in the off-season to supplement their incomes. It would be hard to imagine today's pro athletes needing to drum up off-season work to make ends meet. (Though perhaps some should, given the high rate of bankruptcy reported among former professional athletes.)

The proliferation of organized youth sports appears to follow the upward spiral of athletes' salaries. Although few parents readily admit they want their child to become a professional athlete, parental involvement in youth sports began to increase around the time athletes began receiving ridiculous salaries, particularly in the highest-dollar pro sports—football, baseball, and basketball. The popularity of youth sports has mushroomed in the past two decades, a timeline that parallels skyrocketing professional athletes' salaries. While parents may not want to admit it, or even be aware of it, if professional sports returned to the days of blue-collar wages, I'm convinced that a good deal of sanity would be restored to youth sports. Before athletes were making millions of dollars on the field, few people acted out of control when it came to youth sports.

Fear

Abductions of children have decreased over the past several years. During this same period of time, parents' fears about their children being abducted has seemingly increased. As a parent, one of my greatest fears is a tragedy happening to Jack or Adam. The downside to these fears is that parents can become overprotective to the point that while kids might be slightly safer, society may be worse off as a result. Fear has led parents to restrict their children from going to parks and recreation centers during the day. In fact, these rec centers may actually be more dangerous because they are less crowded.

Jacob Wetterling was just eleven years old when he was abducted in 1989 near St. Cloud, Minnesota. He was never found, but even today, police search for clues and the story remains in Minnesota's news. As tragic as the story is, it's at least somewhat reassuring to remember that if disappearances of this kind were a more common occurrence, Jacob's story would be less likely to receive media attention more than two decades later.

Fear for our children has led parents to demand more organized sports. While there are some positive aspects to this approach to youth sports, it reduces the likelihood that kids will spontaneously go to the park to form their own games.

Conformity

When some parents decide parks aren't safe for their children, other parents often follow suit. Before long, even more parents come to the same conclusion. Soon, only a few children may remain at the park, and their parents may now feel that without more kids around, the park isn't safe. Also, the kids who are still allowed to go the park may be less interested in the absence of some of their other friends. Thus, fear can lead individual parents to make decisions that can trigger conformity in other parents. We typically conform for one of two reasons: to fit in or to make good decisions. When we see other parents sign their children up for multiple teams in multiple sports, one natural reaction is for us to follow suit and do the same.

The Scorecard of Parenthood

On the days when each of my sons were born, I was acutely reminded of my responsibilities as a father. It's unlike any other feeling in the world. Most of us are well-intentioned parents, so we want the best for our children. We also come to view our children as a reflection of ourselves. As a result, it's easy to find our egos wrapped up in child rearing. Whether it's feeling embarrassed at the grocery store because your kids are whining, in front of friends because of different disciplinary styles, or in front of a teacher because of your child's misbehavior in school, it's easy to feel as if your children's mistakes are your own. In the same way, parents often take pride in their children's accomplishments. Of course, this can also be dangerous. I imagine we're all aware of parents who live vicariously through their children, a distressing situation with a number of serious hazards, including added pressure to the child, an increased likelihood of the child being overwhelmed and burned out, and parental frustration because they're not in control of their children's performance. Even if the child manages to perform well, it's sad when a parent's existence centers around a youth baseball or basketball team.

One of the reasons parents' egos get more involved in sports than in other areas is that sports have scoreboards, often very public ones. In school, students who get outstanding grades may be recognized in a newsletter, on the dean's list, or in a school assembly, all of which tend to occur once or twice per year. Even then few specifics are given surrounding those children's performances; it's only known that they surpassed some standard. In addition, rarely would a student be recognized in front of other parents. On the negative side of the ledger, if a child misbehaves in school, word may spread through the rumor mill, but it's unlikely that the student's actions would be publicized.

In sum, rarely are children singled out publicly for positive behavior, and even less frequently for negative behavior.

In the world of youth sports, however, kids' actions, accomplishments, and failures are there for everyone to see, day after day and play after play. One of the consequences of parental involvement is that parents watch many of the games their kids play. That means many parents know if Billy has been in a hitting slump, if Jenny has been struggling with her shooting, or if Tommy made a mistake that allowed the winning goal. Thus, children may feel their performance is being evaluated and monitored not just by teachers and their parents, as with school, but also by their peers and other parents. Instead of playing, children are performing, which can undermine one of the major goals of sports. This shift from playing to performing affects both children and parents negatively. Most children don't take math exams with dozens of parents watching, cheering, hollering, encouraging, yelling, or even criticizing the performance. Imagine how odd it would be to see parents show up for exams in school and then spend hours dissecting their child's performance at home. Why then, do we accept those same behaviors as normal for WOSPs at sporting events?

Parents as Coaches

Talk to any coach who has coached his or her own child and you'll hear story after story of conflicts with parents and other players. Playing time, shots taken, number of innings pitched, and positions played all become points of contention. Just this past week, a friend told me about her eight-year-old daughter's softball team. The coach's daughter is on the team, and she had pitched every inning of the past three games. Parents were unhappy because they felt other children weren't getting an opportunity to develop their pitching skills. There are countless other stories of parents as coaches who consciously or unconsciously provide their child preferential treatment.

My dad was a grade-school basketball coach for twenty-five years. Growing up, I went to all his practices, loved the game of basketball, and dreamed of one day playing for my dad. However, I attended a different school so I played on its team, a rival of the team my dad coached. I regularly asked to transfer schools and my dad's response was always the same: "No." He felt I would learn more from a coach who wasn't also my father, and I would avoid dealing with parents and players who felt he was playing favorites.

Although, I've seen instances in which it worked out well to have kids be coached by their parents. Usually in these cases, the child is very good—to the degree that other parents can't complain about favoritism leading to extra playing time.

I ended up playing for a number of coaches, and learned a lot from each one. Had I played for my dad, I'm certain I would've had a good experience, but I'm less sure it would have prepared me as well for high school and college.

Traveling Teams

When I was in grade school, our teams were primarily school teams, coached by a teacher. Many of the basketball and baseball coaches in our area had coached at the same school for twenty or more years. As a result, there was a certain consistency in the school programs. Furthermore, parents typically didn't interfere much because the coaches had been at the school forever and, at the very least, he or she wasn't going to make decisions based on benefitting his or her own child.

In addition to more parents coaching teams in recent years, a greater emphasis has been placed on traveling and AAU teams and less on school teams. This is unfortunate in the sense that school teams tended to build a strong sense of loyalty among players who worked together for several years. Today, the traveling teams have a sort of "hired gun" approach, with players moving from team to team and program to program too frequently.

A few years back, two former players of mine (Bryan and Mike) started an AAU basketball program. They did a tremendous job of working to develop players' skills, when all too often these AAU teams do nothing but play games. After one two-hour practice in the middle of the summer, Bryan spent an extra ninety minutes working out their top player, Cory, individually. Bryan wasn't being paid to work extra with Cory; he simply wanted to help the player improve. Once the workout was over, Cory left the gym, and ten minutes later sent Bryan a text message letting him know he was joining a different AAU team for the last two tournaments of the summer. He wanted to play on a team that had NCAA Division I recruits on it, so he'd receive more exposure in front of college coaches. Whether this decision would enhance a player's chances of gaining a scholarship is open for debate.

Although Cory would be seen by more college coaches, they wouldn't be there to see him, and he'd get considerably less playing time and fewer shots than on Bryan and Mike's team.

The larger issue, though, is what Cory had been taught about loyalty. He'd committed to Bryan and Mike's team, but backed out when a better opportunity came along. What kind of precedent does this set for Cory in terms of other difficult decisions in life? If one of the potential lessons learned through sports is loyalty to one's team, jumping from team to team seems counterproductive. Would he have been better served by spending more of the summer working on his individual skills, studying for the ACT exam, and earning money for college and spending less time traveling the country for AAU tournaments?

As a kid I played on a baseball team of twelve-year-olds with a very demanding coach. He fined us if our spikes weren't shined, our uniforms were dirty, or if we misbehaved. It was clear at the beginning of the summer that this team was to be our first priority. Imagine my confusion when the playoffs started and this same coach invited several of us to play for an All-Star team that was going out of state to play in a tournament. When I told the coach I was staying with our initial team because he'd talked to us so much about loyalty, I remember him being furious (while I was utterly confused) that I wasn't coming to the out-of-state tournament. The hired-gun mentality in youth sports undermines the loyalty we hope youth sports instill.

Because school teams are perceived as lower in quality and competitiveness, some schools have cut or eliminated budgets for sports. As a result, kids may have no choice but to join a traveling team. Who coaches these traveling teams? Parents—typically WOSPs! These parents don't enter coaching with the goal of being biased toward their children. Often, they're persuaded to help out because a coach is needed. Of course, there are cases when parents are motivated to coach because they think nobody else is suitable for the position. Either way, problems can start as soon as the perception (real or imagined) arises that the coach/parent is biased. In fact, there is virtually no way to avoid this being the case.

Have Parents Changed, or Has the Culture of Sports Changed?

As a college coach, one of the more common questions I get asked is whether kids have changed over the past twenty or thirty years. Meaning, are they softer, less devoted, and more spoiled? These questions assume that kids today don't work as hard as their counterparts several years ago.

Many coaches believe kids have changed for the worse because many of them have been coddled. As a result, these coaches argue, athletes today want constant reinforcement and attention. However, this assertion that kids today don't work hard ignores the fact that kids today have likely spent significantly more hours honing their skills, weight training, and practicing in their sport than their counterparts of thirty or forty years ago. So are kids different today? In some ways, probably yes. But, when it comes to basic needs, our kids have the same ones (food, shelter, love) that kids forty years ago had.

What about parents then? When we examine why parental behavior and involvement in youth sports has changed, it's easy to draw the conclusion that it's actually parents who are different today.

If we consider the amount of parent involvement as our kids' fans, spectators, coaches, and chauffeurs, there's no question that parents today are more involved in youth sports than ever before.

Furthermore, a cursory view of youth sports provides countless examples of parents who have stepped out of bounds on the playing field of parenting. Whether a parent screams at a ref, a child, a coach, or another fan, it stems from a feeling of entitlement and an expected return on their investment. It's easy to conclude that in terms of the time, money, and mental energy they invest in their children's sports careers, today's parents are different than those of previous generations. But that doesn't tell the whole story.

It's difficult to measure change over time and across different samples of people. What evidence would convince us that parents today are different in more fundamental ways? As with children, it seems nearly impossible that evolutionary factors have changed parents over a few decades. So why have parents changed with regards to their involvement in youth sports?

Social Psychology and the Fundamental Attribution Error

Social psychology may hold a key to understanding our perceptions of changes in parents. Two basic principles underlie social psychology. The first is that each one of us perceives the world through our own individual lens, producing a unique subjective perception of reality for each of us. This helps explain why certain behaviors that appear normal to me may appear very strange to someone else.

The second principle is that situations can be powerful, and they can override personality in determining behavior. The fundamental attribution error (FAE) occurs when we overestimate the role of personality, and underestimate the power of situational factors in determining the causes of behavior. Thus, a parent may be perfectly sane, but act crazy due to cultural factors. With respect to youth sports, the

FAE predicts that we will tend to attribute this outlandish parental behavior to crazy parents, as opposed to a crazy sports culture.

Parental Behavior Is as Shocking as Milgram's Studies of Obedience

The most famous study in the history of the field of psychology was conducted by psychologist Stanley Milgram (1933–84): the experiment on obedience to authority figures, commonly called the Milgram Shock Experiment. Milgram was a psychology professor at Yale University who wanted to understand Nazi Germany, the evil regime of Adolf Hitler, and obedience to authority. To understand the nature of evil people, Milgram designed a study in which the participants (the teachers) were instructed to shock another person (the learner) each time that other individual made a mistake on a word-association test.

For the first mistake, participants were instructed to administer a shock of fifteen volts, and they were to increase the voltage of the shocks by fifteen volts for each subsequent mistake. There were a total of thirty shock levers on the machine, which were labeled as fifteen to 450 volts. Along with the voltage numbers, the machine also contained descriptions of the volts, such as "mild," "moderate," "severe," "danger," and "XXX." Unknown to the participant-teacher in charge of administering the shocks, the learner was actually an accomplice of Milgram's (a confederate) who didn't actually receive the shocks. To make this believable, Milgram administered a mild shock to each teacher, placed them in a separate room from the learner, and then played an audiotape of the confederate screaming in pain due to the supposed shocks.

As the screaming got louder, many participants became quite

uncomfortable and asked to stop the experiment. Milgram gave them commands including, "You must continue," and "You have no other choice, you must go on." Participants had to refuse Milgram's commands to continue four consecutive times for the experiment to end.

Milgram predicted that virtually nobody would go all the way to 450 volts. In fact, Milgram thought this study would be his "control condition" for future studies because he thought obedience levels would be incredibly low in this initial study. When he polled psychiatrists, they predicted only one in one thousand (0.10 percent) of participants would reach the maximum voltage. In subsequent studies, he planned to increase the pressure placed on participants by an authority figure. Milgram conducted a poll of psychiatrists, and they shared his prediction that only 0.10 percent of the population would shock another person all the way to the experiment maximum of 450 volts. When Milgram asked college students to predict the results, their average response was that participants would reach 120 volts and then refuse to continue.

What did Milgram's experiment show? Although participants were clearly distressed during the study, with most asking to leave the study, a staggering 65 percent of participants went all the way to 450 volts! Furthermore, the average shock level participants administered was 370 volts. Milgram was shocked by these results. He had predicted that none of the forty participants would obey to 450 volts. Books have been written about the numerous factors that conspired to produce these stunning results. The fact that the study took part at Yale, that they couldn't see the person they were shocking, that Milgram was a legitimate authority figure, and that the shocks started small (only fifteen volts) and gradually increased all played a role in the enormous display of obedience. In his future work, Milgram modified variables such as the prestige of the institution, the legitimacy of authority, and whether or not other participants went along with Milgram's commands. In those later modified experiments, obedience ranged from zero to 93 percent, depending on the variation of the study. The high level of shocks in Milgram's initial study combined with the tremendous variability in obedience in the different variations of the study highlight the powerful role situational variables exert on our behavior.

There are several important take-home messages from Milgram's studies, but situational power is most relevant to our discussion of youth sports parents. Milgram's studies of obedience show that obedience to authority can vary tremendously, depending on a host of situational factors. Milgram described one participant who was relaxed at the outset of the study, and within a mere twenty minutes, the man was "reduced to a twitching, stuttering wreck." Similarly, the youth sports culture has a powerful impact on well-intentioned parents who want the best for their children yet within a mere twenty minutes can be reduced to WOSPs of the worst kind. Before they know what hit them, parents can become overinvolved, can overinvest in terms of time and money, and can put pressure on their children to perform.

Milgram's studies are stark illustrations of the fundamental attribution error, i.e., underestimating the role of situational factors. At first glance, it's natural to assume that the participants in Milgram's studies who thought they were shocking an innocent stranger with 450 volts (enough to kill someone) must have been sadists. However, it's important to note that Milgram had done background checks and psychological testing on participants and excluded them from the study if they had either a criminal history or a psychological disorder. Essentially, Milgram's participants were representative of the average population. They weren't sadists or criminals, which makes the study that much more frightening because it suggests that any one of us might have done the same. The results imply that the participants' choice was less about them as people and more about the power of the situation.

With respect to parental behavior in youth sports, we find a similar set of circumstances. If we simply look at the most egregious examples of parental behavior, the culture of youth sports seems less dangerous. However, if parents who go overboard at youth sports are just like you and me, then we're left to confront the reality that given the right combination of circumstances, we too could be those problematic parents.

When we engage in the fundamental attribution error, we ignore the powerful role that a culture plays in shaping behavior. To what extent does our culture shape parental behavior in sports? Are parents who go overboard crazy?

Milgram conducted one version of his study in which participants were allowed to determine the level of shock to administer, with no pressure from an experimenter. The results? Not a single participant went all the way to 450 volts. In that version of the experiment, the average was 120 volts. Essentially, when strong situational pressure was removed, participants' behavior was guided by their personal values. In the same way, the complex culture of youth sports creates a powerful situation that makes it difficult for parents to remain true to their values.

Of course, it's naïve to think these changes have all taken place in the last couple decades. As with most social change, shifts in behavior occur far more gradually than we might expect. In fact, in the same way that Milgram's participants wouldn't have shocked the learner-confederate at 450 volts to begin the study, incremental changes tend to go unnoticed until it is too late. Change in the culture of youth sports has been gradual, and is not a completely new phenomenon.

In 1973, legendary Penn State University football coach Joe

Paterno observed, "Whatever happened to the good old days when if you felt like playing baseball you would round up your buddies, get a bat and a ball, and would go out and play? What do we do now? We dress up our kids in uniforms, give them professional equipment, tell them where to play, when to play, organize their games for them, give them officials, and put them in the hands of a coach who does not know the first thing about the sport or what's good for an eight-year-old."[9] It's scary to consider that if Paterno observed this phenomenon forty years ago, imagine how far removed youth sports is now from where it began. The wind has been blowing this way for decades, but now those winds of change may be causing more recognizable damage to young athletes and their parents.

Though we recognize that situational variables can have a powerful effect on behavior, we shouldn't excuse WOSPs for unruly behavior. It's important to understand how youth sports have changed and evolved, how an increased pressure has developed for parents to be involved, and how being overinvolved can lead to a vicious cycle of parental investment, cognitive dissonance, frustration, and burnout among young athletes. Our job as parents is to help create an environment that encourages our children to learn important lessons from sports, and in which young athletes are motivated and challenged both physically and mentally. Youth sports have come a long way from their early days—with more organization, and more structure, they require higher levels of commitment and investment than ever before. Subsequent chapters explore why parents have become more involved in youth sports, and whether these changes in youth sports are beneficial for our children.

---

9.   Arnold LeUnes and Jack R. Nation, *Sports Psychology*, 3rd ed. (Pacific Grove, CA: Wadsworth, 2002), 342.

Words of Wisdom for WOSPs

1. Keep in mind the original goals of youth sports: Keep kids active, challenge them, teach them valuable lessons, and keep them busy and out of trouble by providing positive activities. Periodically assess through reflection and discussion with your children whether these goals are being met.

2. Evaluate which goals of youth sports are most important to your child. What are the most important goals of youth sports to you? Do these goals match? Seek first to understand your child's goals, then to have your goals be understood by your child.

3. Be careful when judging other parents' behavior. We are all products of our culture. Don't assume you're impervious to the powerful cultural effects of youth sports. Ask trusted friends and family (including your child) to openly and honestly evaluate your parental behavior as it relates to youth sports. It is easy for each of us to get swept up—and occasionally swept away—by the culture of youth sports, so having forthright feedback about your participation can help keep you anchored.

3

Parents' Need for Children to Feel Good: A Breeding Ground for WOSPs

Humans like to feel good. In fact, seeking out pleasure is a basic drive inside of all of us. Actions that bring pleasure (and avoid pain) contribute to our survival. So it makes sense that we seek out these experiences. This drive to feel good is also visible in parents' desire to see their children experience pleasure and avoid pain.

The desire to feel good affects our behavior in a number of ways. It affects our choices—our activities, the people with whom we spend our time, and even what we think about during our downtime. I believe one of the reasons outlandish behavior from parents receives so much attention is that, in a twisted way, their egregious acts allow the rest of us to feel better about ourselves. When we read about a father attacking an umpire, or a mother criticizing the coach for not playing her child more, we can smile and think, "I'd never be that parent!" We may also use downward social comparisons (comparing ourselves to others and judging ourselves better in some domain) when we hear about extreme involvement in youth sports. Take the parent who spends most of his free time organizing out-of-town tournaments that consume most of his family's weekends. In these cases, parents are still likely to claim that, "I'm not as bad as that other parent. I just want what's best for my child." The process of downward social comparison is a natural one that quickly and effectively allows us to restore positive feelings about ourselves. But that can be a slippery slope because it releases us from a need to be self-critical in areas where an honest appraisal of our performance may be necessary for self-improvement.

I experienced this social comparison a few years back when I received a call from Jim, a longtime friend of mine. Jim and I grew up playing basketball and baseball together in high school, and basketball in college. We were fortunate to play on a state-tournament team in basketball, a state-championship team in baseball, and a Division III Final Four team in college. Jim, who has always possessed the quiet competitiveness of a champion, is now a successful attorney working for a well-respected law firm in Minneapolis.

Jim is also a wonderful dad who wants each of his four kids to have every opportunity to be happy and successful. A number of years ago, Jim called me to alert me to T-ball sign-ups the coming Monday. I was initially hesitant because the sign-ups coincided with the 2005 National Championship basketball game featuring North Carolina versus Illinois. I quickly came to my senses and realized that certainly my older son Jack should come before a basketball game that would have no direct impact on our lives. As Jim and I talked, we jokingly predicted that our sons would play second and third bases, as we had, and would form the best right side of an infield since our Cretin-Derham baseball team in 1990. Jim reminded me that kids had to be three years old to play, which meant my son Jack missed the cutoff by one month. We discussed ways to skirt this rule so Jack could play T-ball.

I was beginning to feel a rush of adrenaline, convinced I had a way to make my son the anti-Danny Almonte (the pitcher who led his team to the 2001 Little League World Series after his parents lied about his age to allow him to play with younger children). Then I caught myself and realized that in my excitement to groom Jack as the next Joe Mauer, I neglected to even consider whether it's a good idea to have a two-year-old play T-ball! My questions for Jim shifted from how we'd sneak my son into this league to whether or not the kids would learn anything of value. Jim's daughter Abby had played T-ball the previous summer, and he assured me it was about kids having fun and learning a bit about the game. In the end, I signed up Jack for the league. Not surprisingly, the T-ball wasn't very high quality—the kids spent more time fighting for the ball than catching it, and the highlight of the children's nights were the postgame popsicles. I'm still not sure the kids learned anything about sports, but they did learn how to shake hands after the game and form a straight line for refreshments.

During the action-packed T-ball games, I had plenty of time to ponder a question that continued to plague me. Why had I been so quickly intrigued by Jim's offer to help my two-year-old play T-ball? I thought giving Jack an extra edge when he was two years old would give him an advantage over kids and that extra edge would pay dividends when he was older. I was engaging in downward social comparison, making myself feel good about my son's potential, rather than asking the crucial questions of why. Although it is sometimes counterintuitive, we are also capable of engaging in upward social comparison—comparing ourselves to someone better, which typically results in us feeling worse but then setting higher goals for ourselves. Too often, we ask the *who, what, when,* and *how* questions, but we fail to probe to the deepest level to ask *why,* because we worry about where that will lead us.

I now teach an upper-level psychology course in the study of motivation, and this question—*why?*—is one we ask repeatedly. When exploring motivated behavior ranging from academics to relationships to athletics, understanding the underlying motivation requires a careful analysis of why someone acted in a certain way. This isn't always a comfortable process for students, or most of us. Our culture encourages a fast-paced life that doesn't provide ample time to reflect on the underpinnings of human behavior. Understanding why parents behave the way they do will be critical for us to understand the good and bad of youth sports.

How to Get to the Why

In the course I teach on motivation, I ask students to identify an activity that's highly motivating for them and then explain why this is the case. A typical response early in the semester is: "I like to play the guitar because it's fun." While the statement may be true, it fails to closely examine why playing the guitar is so meaningful. Playing basketball has been a passion of mine since I was four years old. I provide my students with this example, and allow them to ask me questions to ascertain why basketball, and not skipping rocks, skateboarding, or skiing became my hobby. As they ask questions and peel back the layers of my reasons for playing, it becomes clear that ultimately, most of our motivated behavior comes back to two major needs, both of which can be tied to survival: (1) feeling good, which promotes feelings of safety and comfort, thus increasing the likelihood of our survival; and (2) feeling competent, thus increasing the chances we will thrive in our environment, which can also be tied back to survival.

Think about an activity that is highly motivating for you. Why is it easy for you to work hard and invest in this activity? In my case, I played basketball because it was fun for me, but that wasn't the only reason I played. I've often pondered why I find basketball so enjoyable.

As a child, I was introduced to the game by my father, who coached for twenty-five years at a local grade school. All winter, my dad would come home from work about five-thirty each evening, eat dinner, and then head off to practice at six-fifteen. When I was six years old, I began accompanying him to practice. Clearly, part of my passion for basketball came from opportunities to spend time with my dad. The association I formed between spending time with him and basketball was a positive one. Second, I was never forced to play basketball. I was given the option to play, and I was never coerced into attending practices. In fact, I had to earn the right to attend my dad's team practices. If I hadn't done my homework by six o'clock, I didn't get to go. Thus, playing basketball became the incentive that encouraged me to be diligent with my homework. Third, I had some modicum of skill, and the feeling of competence I had when I was playing basketball was an important motivator. Fourth, I met many of my closest friends on the basketball court—and a good number of them remain my good friends today. Fifth, I was competitive as a child, and playing basketball allowed an opportunity for me to channel this competitive drive, while also fostering cooperation with my teammates. Sixth, playing basketball helped keep me in good physical condition. Finally, I was fortunate to be on several outstanding teams during grade school, high school (we won the state championship), and college (we made the NCAA Division III Final Four). In sum, my love for the game of basketball developed because it met multiple needs—it helped me feel good about myself, supported my sense of competence, fostered my relationships with others, and encouraged my ability to freely choose my passions.

That's an extended look at the *why* surrounding my participation in basketball. Although lengthy, it begins to uncover the underlying motives for my love of basketball. To this day, the sound of a ball bouncing, the smell of a locker room, or the sight of a dusty gym floor strewn with popcorn the day after a game conjures fond memories for me. The memories we form and habits we develop as children often stay with us through adulthood. For most parents, youth sports provide a vehicle through which they hope their children will feel good about themselves and their success. (And perhaps the parents wish the same for themselves as a by-product.) Although this sounds reasonable, we will see the desire to feel good can cause problems in other areas of life.

Why Parents Get Overly Involved: The Need to Help Our Kids Feel Good

Social psychologists generally agree that most of our actions can be traced to two basic social goals. First, we want to feel good, and second, we want to be good. Rare is the person who doesn't want to both feel good and be good. These desires extend to our children, and are consistent with the sound intentions most parents possess. Rare are the parents who don't want their child to feel good and competent.

Understanding the needs to feel good and be competent is crucial in understanding why some well-intentioned parents act so poorly when it comes to youth sports.

Simply put, parents care about their children. Parents want the best for their children. This is an evolutionary truth that benefits our children and helps ensure our collective survival. It's common to hear a parent with young children say, "I want to give my children all the opportunities I never had." Although it comes out of the best intentions, this is the type of thinking that leads parents to err on the side of protecting children from anything remotely associated with pain, and providing children with every available opportunity. After all, most of us learned tough lessons through experience—lessons that were painful at the time, but led us to grow.

If It Feels Bad, It Must Be Bad: How Band-Aids Stifle Children's Development

Watching their young child cry out in sadness or pain is one of the more difficult experiences for most parents. Humans are hardwired to use facial expressions and vocalizations to communicate. This helps explain why children innately cry when they're in pain, and why parents are so quick to respond. Without this hardwired communication system, babies would be left unable to indicate when they're hungry, have an upset stomach, or have grown bored of watching a third rerun of *Barney*. As parents, we become attuned to our children's signals, and learn to respond immediately to signs of distress. If we don't respond to our children's needs, we risk the possibility that our kids will develop an insecure attachment to us, not trusting us, and developing anxious interaction patterns.

On the other hand, if we respond to each and every peep, children quickly learn that when they experience the mildest discomfort, they should let out a holler and Mom or Dad will be there to soothe them. When my son Jack was one, he started banging his head when he became very upset. As time passed, his head banging became more frequent. While others thought this was quite humorous, I worried about this little tyke whose head seemed to be harder than the oak floors he was head butting. Each time he did it, someone would rush over to him to make sure he was OK. As time went on, this propensity increased, to the point where it seemed Jack was banging his head over any minor thing that made him unhappy. Typically, it began with something minor, such as someone leaving the room he was in. Jack would express his displeasure by pounding his head against the floor, wall, or an unlucky toy. I began wondering if something was neurologically wrong, as the frequency of his head banging continued to increase.

One day, Jack tried to get my attention by saying, "Da-da-da-da." I was busy working, and I paid little attention to him. He began to bang his head softly against the wall, pausing to look at me for a reaction. He continued head butting the wall with increasing intensity until after five times, he had produced a lump on his head the size of a small egg and he was sobbing uncontrollably. It was at this moment that I realized two things—once Jack put his mind to something, he was very determined, and I had more to do with the head banging than my son did. He had learned that he could get what he wanted by simply inflicting pain upon himself. Those who loved him were in such a rush to prevent him from experiencing any pain, we had failed to realize that with each dash to stop him from head banging, we were reinforcing the very behavior we intended to discourage. Over the next week, I remember feeling considerable anguish in order to extinguish the connection Jack had made between banging his head and receiving warmth and attention. Given the positive response he'd been receiving, the new lack of response to his head banging only prompted him to try harder. He would bang his head harder and harder until he cried; however, hugging him at that moment would only further reinforce the behavior. After a few days of bumps and bruises, he began to learn that there are easier ways to receive love and attention. Most importantly, he learned that head banging wasn't an effective way to gain attention.

So why had good intentions gone awry? Because as parents, we don't like to see our children in pain. I had communicated nonverbally to my son that if he banged his head, he'd get what he wanted. Kids are smarter than we think, and like an accountant conducting a cost-benefit analysis, Jack had learned to weigh the physical costs of banging his head versus the emotional costs of not receiving desired attention.

Although there is a good evolutionary explanation for parents' aversion to their children's pain, social factors play a role as well. In fact, here's where I believe the field of psychology has seen its good intentions go awry. Several decades ago, the self-esteem movement became prevalent in our field, operating under the premise that feeling good is of the utmost importance. Clearly, being happy is not a new goal for humans to pursue. Philosophers have written about the pursuit of pleasure and avoidance of pain for centuries. Like many trends, the pendulum had swung in one direction in the first part of the twentieth century, when raising children to be obedient, hardworking, and disciplined was at the forefront of parents' minds.

As those children grew up, in highly disciplined but not overly nurturing homes, it appears they became committed to raising their children with a focus on self-esteem and happiness. With the increased focus on feeling good, many researchers turned their attention to understanding factors that promote self-esteem. In 1965, sociologist Dr. Morris Rosenberg published his well-known scale that measures self-esteem. Since then, thousands of studies have examined this highly desired but difficult to quantify variable. In the process, countless journal articles, websites, books, and magazines have focused on how each of us can feel better. Go through the checkout line in virtually any supermarket in America and you'll see headlines in the vein of "10 Steps to a Happier You!" and "Feel Good, Every Day, All The Time." We're hardwired to pursue what makes us happy, but these overt reminders that inundate us on a daily basis ensure that happiness is never far from our minds.

As I see it, there are three major problems with this emphasis on self-esteem. First, we're not always aware of what makes us happy. Often, the things we think make us happy (e.g., money and material items) don't have the desired effect. Second, we're often unaware of the things that do strongly correlate with happiness (e.g., simple pleasures, laughter, and relationships). Finally, striving to be happy doesn't ensure that we'll behave in a morally good manner. Striving for happiness doesn't guarantee that we'll get there in the short term or in the long term. Thus, we encounter problems when happiness becomes the end goal, as opposed to a by-product of living a good life. As parents, we take a shortsighted view of our children's development as individuals when we focus on preparing the path for our child, rather than preparing our child for the path. We're all aware that life won't always be easy, and shielding our children from this reality doesn't help them in the long run.

Preparing the Child for the Path, or the Path for the Child?

The self-esteem movement told us that what's best for our child is what feels good. This may work well if we're only concerned with temporary feelings, but if we're focused on the long-term growth of our children, what feels good now may actually run counter to our children's cognitive, social, and physical development. There is no crime in well-intentioned parents wanting what's best for their children. However, when it comes to youth sports, parents are notorious for focusing on a child's feelings at the expense of growth, maturity, and learning. The problem is that growth can be painful. In fact, growth typically is painful.

In *The Prophet* (1923) poet Kahlil Gibran wrote, "Your pain is the breaking of the shell that encloses your understanding." In other words, we must break out of our existing schemas to grow. Humans are able to adapt to all sorts of situations, and children tend to adapt more quickly than adults. Recently, a school near our house underwent a major renovation that affected where kids were dropped off and picked up from school, and where they played during recess. Parents were frenzied with stress of their routine being altered, whereas the children seemed to go about their business without any worries.

So what happens when we're confronted with change, which we often perceive as a new, potentially threatening situation? When we're accustomed to a given environment, our bodies (and minds) operate as if they're on cruise control, making countless predictions based on what we've experienced previously. As soon as a new situation is presented to us, our body's alert system kicks in, telling us that something is different. Now, we can choose to interpret this as an exciting challenge or as a frightening threat. We make this judgment based on the complex combination of our personality, our experiences, and the cues we take from others.

Parents typically experience a jolt of adrenaline when we perceive our children are in danger, which may lead us to become overprotective. In most cases, our children aren't truly in danger, just experiencing some discomfort that may lead them to personal growth, if we'll allow it. Parents' short-term goal of keeping children perpetually happy may be futile—and, in fact, often fails. Below are several stories of WOSPs whose misguided attempts to ensure an excellent experience for their children backfired. In each case, a parent's desire to help avoid a child's temporary pain prevented the child from learning a valuable lesson from sports, the very lessons parents claim they want their children to learn.

There Should Be Rules, Just Not for My Child

On the first day of each basketball camp I direct, I lay out the rules. My goal is to create a fun, enthusiastic, hardworking, and organized atmosphere for learning and playing with as few rules as possible. Kids aren't going to memorize forty rules, nor do I want their focus spent on trying to remember that many. Thus, the overarching rule at my basketball camps is *respect*. Respect teammates, opponents, coaches, referees, equipment, the facility, and themselves. I provide campers with examples of each type of respect so they have a clear sense that we expect them to behave like young adults.

Last summer during a break in camp, a camper kicked a basketball high in the air. Those of you familiar with basketball know that kicking a basketball is right up there with not putting the toilet seat down at home or double-dipping a chip in the office-party salsa: You just don't do it. The basketball flew in the air and ended up landing on another camper's lunch bag, squashing the contents. With peanut butter sandwich blended together with crumbled Oreos and raspberry yogurt, we now had a mess. On the first day of camp, we had discussed kicking a basketball as an example of a violation of the "respect equipment" rule. I told the camper to clean up the mess and then had him run four laps around the gymnasium (approximately three minutes of running).

Later that afternoon, I received a phone call from his mother. She was very displeased that he was told to run laps, stating that he was embarrassed having to run in front of the other campers. I explained that the lesson I hoped he and others learned was that kicking basketballs (or mistreating any equipment) was unacceptable. She proceeded to ask me if I would want my son treated this way if he attended a camp. At the risk of sounding harsh, I told her that if my son broke rules, I would hope there would be consequences—in fact, I'd be disappointed if there weren't. If my child did something wrong, I offered, I would hope he'd feel bad and remember not to do it again. In the end, we agreed to disagree, but it was clear she cared deeply about her son and his welfare. We merely disagreed about how to handle an incident such as this. She wanted her son to avoid consequences that were unpleasant to him, while I didn't think he would learn much unless there was a consequence. I had hoped she would share my view that experiencing consequences for breaking a rule would help him understand the importance of following rules related to safety later in life.

Another rule we discuss at camp is treating other campers with respect. Several years ago at camp, Bill blatantly pushed Tommy in the back, so forcefully that he fell down. Tommy got up slowly, stunned, but not severely injured. I instructed Bill to go sit in the bleachers.

Several minutes later, after I checked on Tommy, I went to talk to Bill about what he'd done. He vehemently denied doing anything wrong. He said Tommy had bumped into him earlier in the drill, and he refused to apologize to Tommy or talk to me further about it. After a couple minutes of trying to engage him, I told him to let me know when he was ready to talk, and that he would sit on the side until we discussed the incident. Ten minutes went by, then twenty, and then thirty. Bill still hadn't moved. I asked him two more times if he was ready to talk. Both times, he refused to respond, so he continued watching from the sidelines for remaining sixty minutes, until camp concluded for the day.

When I checked my voicemail that night, I had a message from Bill's mother, who was irate. She claimed that although my research in psychology was on intrinsic motivation, it was clear to her that all I really did at camp was motivate through fear. The message went on for more than two minutes, and by the end of it, I could feel my blood boiling. I waited ten minutes to calm down a bit, and then called her to clarify what had happened. She began by letting me know how unfair it was to make her son sit out for so long. She continued by saying her son came home and said he wasn't allowed to play because he bumped into another camper. When I asked her if Bill told her that after Tommy accidentally bumped into him, Bill had responded by pushing him from behind so forcefully that Tommy fell to the floor, she got quiet.

I went on to detail three other conflicts between Bill and other campers that had taken place that week. I asked if this had ever happened before. Bill's mom sounded sad as she explained that Bill had trouble getting along with kids at school and frequently got into fights. When I explained to her what he'd done, and how I'd told him he had to sit out until he discussed the situation, she got quiet again. Again,

Bill's mom clearly loves and cares for her son, but her good intentions made it difficult for her to hold him accountable for his actions. Rather than talking to Bill about his actions, Bill's mom tried to excuse his behavior. Undoubtedly this happened repeatedly and Bill learned a powerful lesson: Nothing I do is my fault. Unfortunately, that thinking won't help him in his interactions with friends, teammates, teachers, and coaches.

Work Children Hard, as Long as They're Not Uncomfortable

Most parents claim they want sports to teach their children a good work ethic. However, we live in a culture that promotes comfort and convenience at all costs. The vast majority of societal changes over the past century have been created with improved speed and efficiency in mind. Cell phones, email, the Internet, fast food, thirty-minute pizza delivery, microwaves, groceries delivered to our doorstep—they all keep the world at our fingertips, teasing us with the possibility that we'll never have to leave the confines of our home. We can have food delivered, shop, pay bills, and access countless news sources online; we can play video games and rent movies, all without leaving home. With all of these conveniences, it's easy for kids to find ample entertainment without leaving the cushions of their couches. In other words, working hard takes more work for kids today. Forty years ago, if kids wanted to play, it was either board games inside or ball games outside. Now, virtual reality and interactive video technology like the Wii make video games seem frighteningly close to the real thing. The only problem is that, in most cases, kids are interacting with a computer instead of their peers, and exercising their thumb on a joystick instead of their legs on a soccer field. In a sad commentary on the ubiquity of video games, one state recently spent $35,000 to provide video games that encourage physical activity for phys-ed classes!

This past summer at camp, Jeremy was an eleven-year-old camper who was a relative novice at basketball, rather uncoordinated, and not friendly with the other participants. Not surprisingly, Jeremy struggled to get along with the other campers. When other players came near him, Jeremy invariably became upset and pushed the other players quite forcefully. In essence, he was turning basketball into football. This happened numerous times throughout the day, and I had several conversations with Jeremy. His perception was that other kids were tackling, tripping, or pushing him and he felt the referees weren't making calls that should have been made. From an outsider's perspective, it was clear that Jeremy was tripping over his own feet, the basketball, or just falling from being off-balance. It was also clear he had very little experience playing basketball and he wasn't physically fit. I struggled with how to make the experience better for him. I was surprised then, when I received a message from Jeremy's father that evening, telling me, "Jeremy is really upset about the camp today. I'm calling to ask you a few questions about how you're conducting the camp. I'm interested in the breaks—he said he only had three minutes of breaks over three hours, and he doesn't want to continue with the camp. If he's only getting three minutes of breaks, I'm not sure how that would be fun."

This was a surprising report, because during camps we provide kids a break every twenty to thirty minutes. So Jeremy would have had between six and eight breaks over the course of the three-hour camp. I asked Jeremy's father how Jeremy got along with others.

"Well, he actually gets into a lot of conflicts, both physical and verbal. Just tonight, he came home from camp and got in a fight outside with a neighbor boy."

As I explained the way camp was set up with frequent breaks, Jeremy's father responded, "I'm sorry for calling. Jeremy often makes things up and I should know better than to listen to him."

Clearly, Jeremy's father is in a tough spot, because his need to help his son feel good is in conflict with doing what he thinks is right. Fortunately, he seemed to realize that Jeremy needed to work on getting along better with others. They have a tough road ahead because changing his behavior will require Jeremy to acknowledge that there's a problem and then work to change his habits.

Fear and the Avoidance of Pain: How the Media Capitalizes on Our Evolved Tendencies

One reason parents are so careful connects to their fear for their children's safety. The media does an exceptional job of publicizing tragic stories—e.g., stranger abductions, deaths due to heat exhaustion, and serial killers, to name just a few. As horrific as they are, a large body of research indicates that media coverage of these events leads us to grossly overestimate the likelihood that our own children will be abducted by a stranger, die of heat exhaustion, or be attacked by a serial killer. These are unquestionable tragedies, but I believe the media should spend much more time publicizing other societal problems that pose a present danger to many children, such as childhood obesity, which predisposes children to diabetes and heart disease.

In July 2001, Korey Stringer was entering his seventh season as an offensive lineman for the Minnesota Vikings. He was coming off a Pro

Bowl season, and claimed he was in the best shape of his life. On the second day of training camp, a day with stifling humidity and ninety-degree temperatures, Stringer began struggling after a two-hour practice. He was rushed to the hospital, where they discovered his temperature had risen to 108.8 degrees. Within fifteen hours, Stringer was dead, leaving behind his wife and son. This tragedy became a lightning rod for media coverage. Why did Stringer die? Was it his weight (335 pounds or more)? The heat? The humidity? Stringer's competitive streak? (After being unable to complete the first practice of training camp, Stringer had insisted on finishing the second day.) Was it a symptom of the culture of pro sports? Did trainers monitor him closely enough?

With countless possible explanations, story after story emerged. Local and national news reports discussed factors that lead to heatstroke and how it can be prevented. Stringer's story was a preventable tragedy, and the amount of attention given to heatstroke quickly increased.

A closer look at Stringer's death and the risks associated with NFL training camps revealed that Stringer's death was the first in an NFL training camp in more than twenty years. With thirty-two teams, during twenty years, throughout twenty practices per team, and including approximately sixty players per roster, that means the odds of a player dying in training camp are about one every 720,000 practices. This statistic doesn't minimize Stringer's death, but rather starkly inspires the question: Does the media lead people to fear the things that they should? Put another way, what are the most pressing health concerns in our society, and do these concerns receive adequate media coverage?

In his book, *The Culture of Fear: Why Americans Are Afraid of the Wrong Things* (2000), Barry Glassner provides an overview of humans' irrational fears. For example, my mother frequently tells me how much more dangerous the world is today than when I was growing up. However, the data don't necessarily bear that out; in fact, the data indicate that many crimes are less prevalent today than they were in the 1980s and early 1990s. The availability heuristic helps us understand why people tend to make judgments based on examples that come quickly to mind. Thus, whenever a murder occurs, neighborhoods and cities typically become convinced that things are much more dangerous than they used to be.

In addition to images that spring quickly to mind, many of our fears are evolutionary in nature, which helps explain why we fear snakes, spiders, and heights. Those who lived thousands of years ago and didn't fear those snakes, spiders, and heights were more likely to take risks and therefore less likely to get a chance to reproduce and pass along their genes. So we continue to have fears hardwired inside of us while statistics tell us that Americans' life expectancies have nearly doubled in the last one hundred years. Clearly, we have fewer survival challenges than our nineteenth-century counterparts. However, media images can trigger our evolved tendencies to fear certain stimuli, while we're far less likely to fear potential dangers such as lack of exercise, poor diet, or smoking. While cognitively we know we should eat well, exercise, and avoid smoking, few of us have a strong visceral reaction to the Marlboro Man, whereas a small spider in our house will send many of us shrieking as we search for the nearest shoe to terminate the deadly arachnid.

News programs do the public a disservice when they cover extreme or unusual deaths and injuries while neglecting the actual dangers in our society. While cases of road rage or arson are frightening, they certainly pose a smaller health risk than obesity or heart disease. Picture for a moment what news broadcasts would be like if the story of every person who died of an illness related to smoking or a poor diet was told? Imagine story after story detailing deaths due to these factors. At some point, we'd likely learn to fear those apparently mundane things (e.g., obesity and smoking) that are most dangerous to us.

As parents, we're warned about cribs, toys, paint, heat, lakes, rivers, swimming pools, raw meat, and virtually everything else under the sun—including the sun. At what point do all these warnings add so much stress to our lives that they diminish our quality of life and even affect our health?

Last summer, I had several phone calls from campers' parents complaining about the excessive heat. Actually, I don't think they expected me to do anything about the heat, but they were unhappy because one of the gymnasiums campers play in isn't air-conditioned and gets very hot on summer days. As a result, we try to keep kids in the gym for no longer than forty-five minutes, provide them with spray bottles, and remind them that they can get a drink whenever they want. Even then, I receive phone calls from parents of children who complain about the heat. I imagine there are two possible sources of these complaints. One possibility is that the heat is simply unbearable. However, the vast majority of campers don't complain. Another possibility is that the heat does make things uncomfortable for those kids who are rarely pushed out of their comfort zone. Not coincidentally, each camper who had a parent call to complain about the temperature in the gymnasium wasn't passionate about basketball. I've never had a call from the gym rat's parent, the child who goes and goes like the Energizer Bunny on a basketball court. Calls about unpleasant conditions in the gym always come from the parent of the child who wants to sit out drills regardless of the temperature.

Several summers ago, I received a call from a mom who was

concerned with the ninety-degree weather and lack of air-conditioning during a three-hour afternoon camp. She told me, "Our kids only play in air-conditioned gyms where we live."

I explained that it would be difficult to install AC before the week was over, but that cooler temperatures were on the horizon. I encouraged her son to return to camp the next day.

She responded by asking, "Would you allow your children to play in this heat?"

When I told her my three-year-old son Jack had been going to a camp earlier in the day at the same gym, playing with six- and seven-year-olds, she got quiet. I emphasized that we take great pains to make sure the children are hydrated and get sufficient rest. The heat can be very dangerous, but we also know that inactivity for children is a far greater threat than heatstroke.

Another mother called to complain about the intense heat, claiming her fourteen-year-old was too hot to play. Again, this was a young man my coaches told me refused to expend effort during camp. I wanted to confirm whether or not their report was accurate, so I gave all forty players in his age group the choice to play in the air-conditioned gym, but they'd have to sit out some games, or to go to the hot gym, affectionately known among the campers as the hot box. Thirty-nine of the forty kids said they'd rather play more and go to the hot gym. You can guess the one who didn't. When I shared this story with his mother, she initially defended her son as a hard worker who loves basketball, though she did work her way to acknowledging that he needs to get serious if he wants to play high school basketball. Unless her son changes his habits, his basketball career will end abruptly in high school.

"All Children Should Get Equal Playing Time"

Not surprisingly, these words are typically spoken by a parent whose child isn't a starting player. Although most parents claim they want their kids to learn valuable lessons and improve their skills, playing time is unquestionably the biggest source of frustration for parents. It's always interesting to hear parents' point of view on how coaches should substitute players in and out in youth sports. There are two opposing schools of thought—everyone should play equally versus the best players should play the majority of the minutes. There's a close correlation between a parent's attitude on this issue and the amount of playing time his or her child is receiving. Invariably, if a parent is complaining that the coach substitutes too much, you can be assured that parent's child is one of the top players on the team. Never have I heard a parent exclaim, "My child is playing too much!" It's also common to hear parents of children who aren't getting much court time to recommend the coach play more players. Logically, both positions can't be right. It's a classic case of a self-serving bias, meaning we tend to take credit for our own successes and blame others for our failures. Parents of young athletes are no different. If parents can distance themselves emotionally from how much their child is playing and help their child understand why they are or are not getting lots of playing time, they will be doing their children a tremendous service.

Sadly, this type of parental behavior helps us understand why so many youth sports coaches are driven away from coaching. When I was growing up, my grade-school basketball team primarily played against other schools throughout Saint Paul. In particular, we had a rivalry with four schools within a five-mile radius. Each of those four schools had coaches who had been there for more than twenty years. These were coaches who had dedicated a large portion of their careers to working with young people for virtually no money. Today, those same schools all have exceedingly high rates of coaching turnover. In most cases, the coach is either a teacher at the school who coaches out of necessity or, more likely, a parent who coaches for a couple years while his or her child is on the team. This lack of consistency makes a big difference in the experience. When you ask coaches why they stopped coaching, a common reason is that they're tired of dealing with parents. Most departing coaches will comment that they still love working with the kids, but the parents simply take too much energy.

One of the downsides of coaches quitting is that it increases the likelihood of parents serving as coaches. This usually means teams are led by novices who can't be completely objective in difficult situations. No matter what their decision, it will be difficult to convince another parent that a parent-coach is unbiased and fair with all players. The resulting skepticism can serve as a trigger for bad parental behavior at youth sporting events.

In the end, all of these stories involve parents who are concerned—I believe too concerned—with their child's feelings. An overabundance of concern causes them to lose sight of the central goals of sports: development of discipline, work ethic, teamwork, and resilience. In fact, most of the lessons we learn in life, we learn from painful experiences.

From Pain Comes Growth

I was fortunate to play on some very successful teams throughout my high school and college career. In high school, our basketball team qualified for the state tournament my junior year and we won the state championship my senior year, and our baseball team won the state championship my junior year. Several of my basketball teammates earned Division I scholarships, and five of my baseball teammates went on to be selected in the Major League Baseball draft. In college, I played on three conference-champion teams, in three NCAA Division III tournaments, in the Final Four my junior year, and was captain of our team my senior year when we set a school record by winning twenty-seven consecutive games before being upset in the national tournament. For someone who grew up dreaming about sports, I was fortunate to have many of my dreams come true. Each team success was profoundly satisfying and a lot of fun. However, the two most powerful lessons I learned from sports both originated from painful experiences during high school.

The first took place when I was a skinny fifteen-year-old, having just completed my freshman year of high school. My coach, Randy Muetzel, is one of the kindest people I've ever met. He was encouraging, rarely yelled, and always found the best in everyone. After he made us run sprints one day because we weren't listening, he apologized, "There are lots of people in the world who would give anything to be able to run, so using it as a punishment was a poor decision." We all felt incredibly guilty and worked hard for the remainder of the season.

I was talking with Mr. Muetzel at an open gym in June after my freshman year. He asked me if I was aware that I was the best shooter in the entire school. I was both flattered and embarrassed by this compliment, and tried to argue that many of the varsity players were far better shooters than I was. He persisted in his compliment, but then said, "Even though you're the best shooter in the school, you'll probably get cut from the varsity team as a senior if you don't get quicker and stronger."

I felt sick to my stomach after Mr. Muetzel's feedback. I could feel my dream slipping away. My reality had been shaken. How could this coach I respected and trusted tell me something that just challenged the core of my primary goal in life at that point in time? I don't recall saying anything in response, and I went home feeling ill. Was he serious? I had started on every team I'd ever played on. Was his forecast the truth? Might I get cut from the varsity someday?

I looked in the mirror that night. I was six-foot-one and 120 pounds. I was slow. I was weak. And I couldn't jump. My dad always told me, "If you don't like the situation you're in, do something about it." So after moping around the house for a day, I decided to take his advice. I devised a workout in my basement, which I referred to as The Pit, while I fancied myself a basketball-playing Rocky Balboa. I did circuits of jumping up and down the stairs, push-ups, calf raises, shuffle drills, footwork, and sit-ups. I did my routine of drills for one hour each night, and I'd emerge from The Pit dripping in sweat, but feeling a little quicker and stronger each day. For ninety consecutive days, the entire summer, I continued my program, and by the end of it I was noticeably more athletic. I was never going to be the best athlete on the court, but I had improved tremendously and I'd learned a lot about a work ethic in the process. Had Mr. Muetzel not challenged me, I wouldn't have confronted my weaknesses, moved out of my comfort zone, and gone through pain in order to grow. I continued these workouts throughout high school and the experience taught me a great deal about facing a challenge head-on and working toward a difficult goal. It's a lesson I've drawn from repeatedly throughout college and graduate school, in my professional life teaching and coaching, and in raising my two sons.

The second powerful lesson I learned from a painful experience in sports occurred at the end of my junior year of high school. I had continued to rely on my work ethic to seize opportunities, and had been a starting player in state basketball and baseball tournaments. In the state baseball championship, I led off the third inning with a walk. As I stood on first base, the next batter missed a bunt and the catcher tried to pick me off. I dove back and injured my left shoulder in the process. I continued to play the rest of the game, and scored the game-winning run on a hit by future Heisman Trophy–winner and NFL quarterback Chris Weinke. The next day I went to the doctor and found out my shoulder was broken. I was entering the period where college scouts would watch me play and now I was out for the summer. I was depressed, but quickly decided that rather than sulking, I would work on two things all summer long: fixing the form on my jump shot and my leg strength.

Shooting had always been the strongest part of my game, but because I'd been playing basketball at such a young age, I developed some bad habits. One of these was shooting a two-handed shot, a technique that is less consistent and harder to do well than a one-handed shot, where the shooting hand shoots the ball and the off hand guides it. Every day that summer I worked on shooting with one hand. At first, I was unable to shoot with one hand from even five feet. I took thousands of shots each week and by the end of the summer I was making more than 75 percent of my three-point shots with one hand. My second focus of increasing my leg strength took me from being unable to dunk to where I could dunk easily. To cap it off, I dunked in overtime of the state championship to seal the victory. What an unbelievable way to end my high school career, and what powerful lessons I learned about the value of hard work. These lessons about work ethic have carried over into my teaching, research, coaching, and parenting. By experiencing natural consequences, I was able to learn, grow, and become passionate for the right reasons, all the while learning lessons about hard work, discipline, and resilience.

Words of Wisdom for WOSPs

1. From pain comes growth. Provide safe, but challenging, environments for your children to test themselves, to grow, and to learn the benefits of hard work. Think about the lessons your children will learn before intervening. Sometimes the greatest learning stems from a healthy dose of pain.

2. Provide support for children, but don't enable them or make excuses for them. Kids can learn a lot from a coach's feedback if parents support and reinforce feedback geared toward challenge and improvement.

3. Fun comes from satisfaction, meaning, learning, and growth. Fun doesn't come from the avoidance of pain. We should try to structure fun and challenging activities for children that are not too easy, not too difficult, and centered on learning and growth.

4

Does Raising a Prodigy Mean Ruining a Childhood?

The Stories of Todd Marinovich, Andre Agassi, and Tiger Woods

Recall the young, overcommitted athlete we discussed in the first chapter, sound asleep on a summer Saturday morning at 4:00 a.m. until dreams are shattered by the ringing of his alarm clock and his dad hollering, "Wake up!", signaling the consecutive trifecta of hockey, baseball, and soccer practices. For many children in youth sports, the alarm clocks are ringing too early. All too often, parents aren't allowing their children's dreams time to develop naturally, turning enjoyable activities into nightmares.

Before indicting that little boy's parents, though, we must remember that many WOSPs want to simultaneously protect their children from pain and help them be the best they can be. In the previous chapter, we examined the basic human drive to feel good and how it can lead parents to shield children from adversity, even if that adversity might offer valuable life lessons. To understand parental overinvolvement, we need to examine parents' motives for their children to be successful.

In the same way there's nothing inherently wrong with protecting children from pain, there's nothing objectionable in wanting our children to succeed. In fact, these desires for our children to feel good and perform well are both rooted in our evolutionary history. Children who grow up relatively pain free and learn how to successfully navigate their environment are more likely to survive and reproduce. In that respect, it makes lots of sense for parents to protect kids from pain and teach them how to succeed. Success in sports is often believed to translate to a number of other domains in life, making sports success that much more important to many parents. Although parents' goals to see their children succeed in sports is natural, it can lead some parents to become overinvolved in their children's athletic careers.

The Tipping Point for Youth Sports and Parental Overinvolvement

Malcolm Gladwell is one of the most renowned authors of the past decade. In his best sellers *The Tipping Point* (2000), *Blink* (2005), and *Outliers* (2008), Gladwell captures readers' attention and imagination with his vivid stories supported by reams of social science research. In

The Tipping Point, Gladwell explains how dramatic cultural changes can behave like viruses. Rather than demonstrating linear growth, trends in illnesses, crimes, product sales, or cultural fads often mirror the behavior of viruses in that their growth starts gradually and then increases exponentially. In that way, Gladwell argues, many cultural phenomena seem to surprise people with their sudden growth when really what we're witnessing is a tipping point. Sometimes it's difficult to spot the true moment a phenomenon hits its tipping point until well after it has actually occurred. The same is true in youth sports.

At the end of Chapter 2, I shared Joe Paterno's 1973 quote in which he describes his view of how the highly organized structure of youth sports was hampering children's development. The evolution of youth sports has been a gradual one, with older generations bemoaning the changes that have taken place in both youth sports and the parenting of children by subsequent generations of parents. Over the past thirty years, we've witnessed a surge in the numbers of parents who invest extraordinary amounts of time and money to provide their children the best possible opportunity to excel in sports. Although no one event can be solely responsible, I believe the tipping point that dramatically sped up the wheels of parental overinvolvement can be linked to six individuals: three fathers and three sons. The success, attention, prestige, and monetary gain experienced by three young athletes opened parents' eyes around the world to the role parents could play in their children's development and ascension to stardom in professional athletics. These weren't the only three childhood prodigies who received national exposure, but they were three high-profile young athletes who received early-career attention long before it was in vogue to pinpoint the next great athlete.

In 1988, *Sports Illustrated* introduced the nation to Todd Marinovich, star quarterback at Capistrano Valley High School. At the time, high school (and youth) sports hadn't yet exploded on the national scene. Nowadays, one can find ESPN broadcasts of high school football and basketball games, but in 1988, it was unheard of for a major publication such as *Sports Illustrated* to devote significant space to a high school athlete.

Why did *SI* feature Marinovich? Was it because he'd just set the national record for most passing yards with 9,914? Partially, yes, but record-breaking high school athletes come along every year. The real reason Marinovich captivated the public's attention was the way he was raised by his father, former NFL lineman Marv Marinovich. From the day Todd was born, Marv made it his mission to raise Todd to be an NFL quarterback. Marv spent nearly every moment of every day of Todd's childhood engineering the child into what some called "RoboQB." Would Marv's experiment be successful? Some would argue the experiment was doomed from the start because trying to determine a child's career with no input from the child robs him of choice and autonomy. In any case, Marv Marinovich wasn't the only parent who had a vision of turning his son into the next superstar.

Around the same time Todd Marinovich burst into national prominence, the sport of tennis was becoming enthralled with the newest teenage sensation, Andre Agassi. Agassi was raised in Las Vegas, where his father Mike, a former boxer, trained him. From the time he was young, Agassi traveled around the country, wowing crowds as he defeated much older and larger opponents. Agassi's game had flair, and he had the flamboyant hairstyle and sartorial splendor to match. Crowds loved his emotion and energy on the court, and he quickly became a fan favorite. More important, Agassi's game had the substance to match his outsized style. In 1988, at age eighteen, he became the youngest player to accumulate $2 million in earnings, and he ascended to the enviable position of being the third-ranked male tennis player in the world. He qualified for the semifinals of both the French Open and the US Open, two of the four major championships in tennis (he didn't play in the other two that year). Although still a teenager, he'd emerged as America's next great hope to dominate the world of tennis.

Tiger Woods, although only twelve at the time, won the first of four consecutive Junior World Golf Championships in 1988. Tiger had burst onto the national scene a decade earlier, though, as a two-year-old showcased on *The Mike Douglas Show*. On the show, the toddler demonstrated a fluid swing and uncanny putting stroke that was developed through countless hours of practice with his father, Earl Woods. As the audience watched with delight, the youngster beat Bob Hope in a putting contest. By the time he was ten, young Tiger had appeared on countless other shows, including *That's Incredible!* and *The Tonight Show with Johnny Carson*. *Golf Digest* highlighted the prodigy's ability with the headline: "5-Year-Old Tiger: He's Incredible."

For decades, Americans had been introduced to athletes as they ascended to stardom in the professional ranks, typically in their twenties. Two things had changed on the playing field. First, national attention was given to athletes who were younger and younger every year. Second, media attention was focused not just on the athletes, but also on their parents. This was particularly the case when these athletes' parents trained their children in ways that blurred the line between youth sports and a full-time job. Todd Marinovich, Andre Agassi, and Tiger Woods all became national figures both for their athletic successes and the training methods employed by their fathers. Was this national attention the tipping point of parental overinvolvement in youth sports that actually encouraged more parents to follow suit?

An examination of the childhoods of Todd Marinovich, Andre Agassi, and Tiger Woods reveals many similarities in parental (particularly paternal) overinvolvement. All three dads spent incredible amounts of time and money on their sons' athletic endeavors. Marv, Mike, and Earl committed to providing every opportunity for Todd, Andre, and Tiger to be the best in their respective sports. All three dads understood the importance of both physical and mental training. In addition, each was willing to hire experts to teach their sons unique skills. Finally, the three fathers pushed their sons to be the best and—in some cases—probably pushed a bit too hard. However, amidst all those similarities, there are some striking differences that help explain how apparently similar roads paved by their parents led Todd, Andre, and Tiger down such disparate paths.

The Early Years of Todd Marinovich: Control versus Autonomy

Marv Marinovich began engineering Todd's life well before he was born. Trudi (Todd's mom) removed all salt, sugar, and alcohol from her diet during her pregnancy. She also played classical music during her pregnancy in hopes of stimulating Todd's neurons. As soon as Todd was born, he was placed on a diet of raw fruits, vegetables, and milk. Marv began stretching Todd's hamstrings at the ripe old age of one to improve his flexibility. In fact, much of Marv's philosophy on training evolved as a result of his overtraining with weights during his abbreviated NFL career. At one point, Marv could squat more than eleven hundred pounds, but his body soon broke down. To ensure the best for Todd, Marv hired gurus in virtually every area one could imagine (and then some). Todd wasn't allowed to eat fast food or candy. In fact, when he attended birthday parties, he brought along carrot sticks and treats that didn't contain sugar or unrefined white flour. By the time Todd was eight, he was running four miles in thirty-two minutes, an incredible pace for a child.

Although none of these actions is inherently bad, combined, they exemplify an extreme WOSP. Marv was involved in every aspect of Todd's life, hiring specialists to improve every aspect of Todd's mind and body. Coaches worked on his agility, balance, strength, quickness, conditioning, mental toughness, diet, and even his vision. As one friend said in the 1988 *Sports Illustrated* story, "All Marv has done is give up his entire life for Todd."[10]

What was the goal of these sacrifices? What was the payoff? Was it to promote happiness in Todd? Character development? Discipline? Unselfishness? Unfortunately, it was none of those. Marv admitted in the 1988 *SI* article about Todd, "I think I'm a tyrant. But I think you have to be to succeed . . . it's fanatical, but I don't know if you can be a great success without being a fanatic." According to Marv, anything less than perfection was ordinary, and all of Todd's activities were geared toward perfection. Marv said, "To me, the Robo quarterback means the guy has all the equipment. Everything is in sync. Everything balanced. The perfect machine . . . you could never be too good with mechanics of throwing. You can never be too focused, mentally. You can never have too good of vision. You strive for those things."

10. Douglas S. Looney, "Bred to Be a Superstar: Todd Marinovich was groomed from infancy to be a top-notch quarterback," *Sports Illustrated*, February 22, 1988, http://www.si.com/vault/1988/02/22/117185/bred-to-be-a-superstar-todd-marinovich-was-groomed-from-infancy-to-be-a-top-notch-quarterback.

The Early Years of Andre Agassi: Control versus Autonomy, Part II

While Todd Marinovich was throwing thousands of passes and ingesting only the most nutritious foods, Andre Agassi was staring down the throat of a dragon. Andre's father Mike, an Olympic boxer for Iran, was an intense man. Andre recounted stories of his father pulling his car off on the side of the road to beat other motorists who had cut him off or offended him. Mike Agassi was a fiery competitor who decided that he would manufacture a tennis superstar out of Andre. Mike converted a tennis ball machine into what came to be known as the dragon. As Andre wrote in *Open: An Autobiography* (2009),

> When the dragon takes dead aim at me and fires a ball 110 miles an hour, the sound it makes is a bloodcurdling roar. I flinch every time. My father has deliberately made the dragon fearsome. He's given it an extra-long neck of aluminum tubing, and a narrow aluminum head, which recoils like a whip every time the dragon fires. He's also set the dragon on a base several feet high, and moved it flush against the net, so the dragon towers above me. At seven years old I'm small for my age. But when standing before the dragon, I look tiny. Feel tiny. Helpless. (27–28)

Andre's dad screamed at him whenever he missed a shot, even though the tiny seven-year-old was scared to death, hitting more out of fear than any other motivator. His dad calculated that if he hit twenty-five hundred shots per day, he'd hit nearly one million balls per year! Ball after ball, hour after hour, day after day, Andre was faced with the menacing dragon. Sadly, no matter how outstanding Andre was, he knew he'd never be praised. After all, "I take no pride in my reflexes, and I get no credit. It's what I'm supposed to do. Every hit is expected, every miss a crisis" (27).

The Early Years of Tiger Woods: Control versus Autonomy, Part III

In the same way Marv Marinovich and Mike Agassi were instrumental in developing training regimens for their sons, Tiger's parents, and particularly his father Earl, are mentioned prominently in most discussions of factors that contributed to Tiger's prowess. Earl Woods was a standout baseball player at Kansas State University, and was also the first African-American baseball player at the school. He endured some hostility during his career, but demonstrated the same toughness and focus on his goal that Tiger is known for on the golf course. Earl Woods had an opportunity to leave college early to play professional baseball for the Kansas City Monarchs in the Negro Leagues. Although playing pro ball would have satisfied the aspirations of his deceased father, Miles Woods, Earl decided to stay in college to pursue a degree.

After graduation, Earl entered the Army. He married Barbara Hart, and they had three children together. Earl was stationed in Germany, and did a tour of duty in Vietnam. There were several stresses in the marriage, and Earl acknowledged his role in his subsequent divorce from Barbara, and also his neglect in parenting his three children from that marriage. Earl was later stationed in Thailand, where he met Kultida Punsawad. They married and on December 30, 1975, their son was born: Eldrick "Tiger" Woods.

As Tiger was gaining more notoriety for his precocious golf game during the 1980s, Earl was garnering attention for his involvement in Tiger's development. Stories abounded of the kid from California whose dad was spending up to $30,000 a year for Tiger's golf tournaments, lessons, coaches, psychologists, personal trainers, travel, and equipment. Earl Woods wasn't the first, nor was he the only, overinvolved sports parent, but he certainly received the most attention for his efforts to develop golf's next prodigy.

Not surprisingly, Earl's parenting raised some red flags. Why would anyone subject his child to such an intense schedule? Was he forcing Tiger to play? What kind of return on his investment did he expect? What if Tiger burned out? Would he rebel? What would his relationship be like with his parents, particularly with his father? What if he failed to live up to expectations? What if he regretted not having a childhood? What would Tiger be like as an adult? Would he still love golf? Would he still be successful?

What Happened to Todd, Andre, and Tiger?

After high school, Todd Marinovich elected to attend the University of Southern California, traditionally a football powerhouse. It seemed like a fairy tale: hometown kid chooses to stay in southern California and he leads USC to a national title. In fact, *Sports Illustrated* did another feature story, this one focusing on Todd's college choice, another rare occurrence at that time.

After redshirting his first year at USC, Marinovich was in competition for the starting quarterback position the next season. Just before the season started, starting quarterback Pat O'Hara got injured and Marinovich was named the starter. He was USC's first freshman quarterback to start a season opener since World War II.

Expectations for Marinovich were through the roof. Fans expected Todd to complete all of his passes and go undefeated that season. With impossible expectations, criticism of him mounted when the team lost their season opener to the University of Illinois. Marinovich regrouped and lead USC to a 9-2-1 record and a Rose Bowl Championship. *Sporting News* named Marinovich the National Freshman of the Year. He was the first freshman quarterback to be named to the All Pac-10 team. He came within 0.1 percent of setting an all-time NCAA record for completion percentage by a freshman QB. Marinovich had an objectively outstanding freshman season that still didn't appear to equal fans' expectations.

What would it be like to be burdened with the expectation of perfection? In his younger years, Marinovich experienced social anxiety. His coping skills were less than adaptive: he'd been smoking marijuana to relax since high school. Essentially, Marinovich couldn't escape his own shadow, a burden of self-awareness that can be debilitating. At one point in his freshman year, Marinovich visited his mother and said, "I wish I could go somewhere else and be someone else. I don't want to be Todd Marinovich."[11] Here was a college freshman living the dream: attending a football powerhouse, playing starting quarterback as a freshman, recognized as a big man on campus, awarded the freshman of the year award, and leading his team to a Rose Bowl. His future looked as bright as can be, yet he wanted no part of it. How in

---

11. William Plummer, "Todd Marinovich Was Raised for Football Glory, but a Cocaine Bust and a Sacking by His Coach Mar the Dream," *People* 35, no. 5 (February 11, 1991), http://www.people.com/people/archive/article/0,,20114426,00.html.

the world did success become so painful?

How did Todd make sense of his world crashing down on his shoulders? He acknowledges being painfully shy. In fact, he recounts how drinking during high school eased social pressure on him. Todd said, "Partying . . . opened up a new social scene for me—liquid courage. I wasn't scared of people anymore."[12] However, once he appeared on the cover of *Sports Illustrated* in 1988, the monster was unleashed. People from far and wide knew about RoboQB, but the locals knew he wasn't as clean as advertised. By his senior year, opposing fans at basketball games were chanting "Marijuana-vich" at him while he shot free throws. It's as if the first chapter in his life was programmed for him, and in the second chapter he used drugs to escape the pain. By his freshman year at USC, it was clear his father's controlling ways had gotten to him, and that he was enjoying his newfound freedom a bit too much. At the time, Todd said, "I have to discipline myself. I just have to. I'm finally away from my dad telling me everything to do. And I've got to say I've taken advantage of it. Full advantage. He keeps telling me, 'Come on, you've got the rest of your life to fool around. Not now.' I know he's right. But there are a lot of distractions at USC." As two attractive co-eds walked by, he concluded simply, by saying, "See what I mean?"[13]

Marv was clearly frustrated when he compared the freshman Todd to the younger version: "I told him when to eat, what to eat, when to go to bed, when to get up, when to work out, how to work out. Now I have a hard time getting him on the telephone. He seems to be leading a lifestyle that is wearing. The interviews, missing meals, bad sleeping habits. Things are just starting to slip. I told him, 'You are making bad

---

12. Mike Sager, "Todd Marinovich: The Man Who Never Was," *Esquire*, April 23, 2010, http://www.esquire.com/sports/a5720/todd-marinovich-0509/.

13. Looney, *Sports Illustrated*, February 22, 1988.

decisions, but I can't make them for you anymore.' He went directly from an environment where everything was regimented to a totally open door." Although this description sounds strikingly similar to thousands of college freshman around the country each year, Todd's newfound autonomy was channeled in every direction but football. The control Marv had over Todd throughout his childhood had a disastrous effect on Todd's intrinsic motivation to play football.

Eventually, Marinovich was arrested for cocaine use and that was only the beginning of his legal troubles. By the beginning of his third year in the NFL, he had failed three drug tests and was out of professional football. He bounced around the Canadian Football League, where his drug use only intensified—to the point where he was once so high during a game that he told his coach he couldn't enter the game. At last count, Marinovich had been arrested nine times and was regularly seen skateboarding on Newport Beach.

Andre Agassi was one of the greatest tennis players of all time. His accomplishments are too numerous to list here, but among them were wins at all four Grand Slam tournaments plus an Olympic gold medal. Seems like a dream career come true. However, the seven-year-old boy never got over the dragon, nor did the thirteen-year-old boy get over being shipped out to an elite tennis academy in Florida. From the time Andre was a boy, he was groomed to be a tennis star more than he was groomed to be a person.

At the end of his career, Agassi wrote an autobiography in which he recounts his hatred for tennis caused by the intense pressure he felt to succeed from the time he was a child. Number-one ranking in the world, one of the best players in tennis history, more than thirty million dollars in tennis earnings, more than $100 million in endorsements—in the end, Andre may have even surpassed his father's expectations. He had it all: unparalleled success, endless fame and fortune, and the adulation of millions. And he was miserable.

You'd have live in a cave to be unaware of Tiger Woods's accomplishments. Three decades after his appearance on *The Mike Douglas Show*, Woods is one of the few youth prodigies who has lived up to, and exceeded, the hype. He has won seventy-one tournaments, including fourteen major championships. Woods is closing in on Jack Nicklaus's record of eighteen major championships, and it's generally acknowledged that if he breaks Nicklaus's record, he'll vault to the top of the list of golf's all-time great players. Many already consider him to be the greatest golfer of all time. Thousands of articles and numerous books have been written about Tiger's success, and his talent, ambition, work ethic, motivation, and passion are all major factors in it.

Tiger displayed remarkable consistency at a young age. He won the Optimist World Junior Championships at ages eight, nine, twelve, and thirteen. In 1993, he won the US Junior Amateur Championship. In 1994, 1995, and 1996, he became the first golfer to win three consecutive US Amateur Championships. Woods turned pro in 1997 and in his first year on the PGA tour, he was the leading money winner. For the next twelve years, Woods was so dominant that no one even debated who was the world's best golfer. In some tournaments, Woods was considered to have as much as a 50 percent chance to win, which is astonishing given that he was playing against more than one hundred of the world's best golfers!

Woods attained this remarkable status despite constant pressure. His every shot is watched, every swing analyzed, and every reaction scrutinized. In fact, when Woods plays, television ratings are often more than 100 percent higher compared to when he doesn't. Imagine that millions of spectators were watching every shot you hit, expecting perpetual perfection. How did Tiger develop his mind and body to thrive in situations constantly packed with pressure?

Earl Woods admitted a tremendous guilt about the underinvolvement he had with his three children from his first marriage. He also acknowledged overcompensating with Tiger. Similar to Marv Marinovich, Earl was committed to providing every opportunity in the world for Tiger. The difference is that Earl understood that forcing people to do things eventually backfires, and this is a critical difference between how Tiger and Todd were raised, and why they turned out the way they did.

Earl Woods took up golf late in life, and didn't have anywhere near the expertise in golf that Marv Marinovich did in football. However, Earl developed a passion for the game and would play most days after work. Tiger would eagerly call Earl each afternoon, begging to play too. Earl would always pause, as if in deep contemplation, and often feign uncertainty as to whether Tiger would be able to join him. After a couple moments, Earl would relent to Tiger's wishes, which were of course consistent with Earl's as well. Although Tiger didn't realize it, Earl was simply letting Tiger drive the decision to play golf. This was brilliant, because each day Tiger asked to play, he convinced himself that he wanted to golf more than anything else in the world. Had Earl forced him to golf, Tiger wouldn't have had the same intrinsic motivation to play golf.

Many have assumed that Earl forced Tiger into golf. Instead, Earl and Kultida had a keen understanding of how to foster intrinsic motivation. Jay Brunza, a family friend, commented that all Earl and Kultida wanted was to encourage Tiger to pursue his passions. Brunza went on to say, "Tiger was pursuing something from intrinsic passion for the game, and wasn't forced to live out somebody's else's expectations. If he said 'I'm tired of golf, I want to collect stamps,' his parents would say 'Fine, son,' and walk him down to the post office."[14]

---

14. Bill Gutman, *Tiger Woods: A Biography* (New York: Pocket Books, 1997), 28.

Perfection versus Challenge

Marv Marinovich had a vision of the perfect quarterback, an ideal he wanted Todd to attain. His ideal called for efficiency of movement, impeccable mental toughness, and unsurpassed attention to detail. However, a perfectionist attitude can backfire. The problem with perfectionism is that if that's the gold standard—the way you measure success—then when you fail to attain perfection, you've failed completely. This is as true for the individual suffering from alcoholism or an eating disorder, or for the child who feels the burden of parental expectations of perfection. Todd Marinovich felt he would never live up to the expectations of others. Combine that with his social anxiety, and one can imagine the immense pressure he felt from the outside.

How did Tiger excel at such a young age? Part of his success centers on his love for a challenge. Tiger's dad would create games that would tantalize Tiger's desire to excel. In one putting drill, Earl would place golf balls in six-inch increments away from the hole. Every time Tiger made one, he would move back to the next ball. If he missed, he moved up six inches. This is a game he could play by himself or with others, and many believe it's one of the reasons his putting skills are unparalleled. Earl found ways to create optimal challenges for Tiger while teaching him basic fundamentals. When most kids were working on driving the ball three hundred yards, Tiger was working solely on his putting. Gradually, Earl allowed him to work on his chipping, then his iron play, and finally his drives. This attention to the foundational skills of golf helped provide Tiger with an appreciation for details and an ability to create challenges for himself while practicing skills many other kids would have found relatively boring.

In 2010, however, Tiger's marital infidelities became public. What looked like the perfect life now appears to have been a façade. Woods had been cheating on his wife, Elin Nordegren, for several years with numerous women. He took a leave of absence from the PGA Tour, and after his return, he struggled to regain his previous form. It remains to be seen how the rest of Tiger's career will go after the revelations that the image he and his sponsors had crafted was nowhere near reality.

Team versus Individual Sports

One reason Andre Agassi and Tiger Woods were more success-ful than Todd Marinovich may be because they participated in an individual sport. I don't doubt that Andre or Tiger could have been a great quarterback, but that would've required some additional inter-personal skills that are less relevant in tennis or golf. Athletes in indi-vidual sports focus solely on their own game, an attitude that's viewed as selfish on a team. Furthermore, being on a team requires trust and vulnerability. In team sports, Andre and Tiger would've had to build trust with their teammates, who may have struggled to relate because of their superior mental and physical abilities.

Todd Marinovich had to learn how to engage as part of a team at the same time he was developing his elite athletic abilities. Not only was Todd in the media spotlight from a young age, but he was also playing the most pressure-packed position in all of sports: quarter-back. He was in charge of each huddle before each play started. Every-one's eyes were on him at the start of each play. Everyone expected him to make a great play. At the conclusion of the game, he would get the majority of the credit for a win or blame for a loss. Marinovich experienced a tremendous amount of pressure on his shoulders each and every game, and it wore on him over time.

Genetics

Although we don't have access to analysis of Andre's or Todd's or Tiger's DNA profiles, we can be certain their genetic makeup has something to do with their successes (and failures). All three are blessed with hand-eye coordination that allows them to perform in highly specialized ways. During competition, Tiger's eyes take on a steely focus that few seem to possess. Although it's a skill he cultivated, it's unlikely many people have the capacity to focus in such an intense fashion while maintaining their composure.

In 2010, a reporter asked Todd if he finally stopped using drugs because he no longer had to escape the pressure of being a professional athlete. Marinovich struggled to answer the question, before answering: "I think more than anything, it's genetic. I got that gene from the Fertigs (his mom's side of the family)—my uncle, the Chief. They were huge drinkers. And then the environment plays a part in it, for sure."[15] Todd Marinovich was the perfect blend of nature and nurture that conspired to produce an overtrained, stressed-out, and burned-out young athlete.

Unconditional Positive Regard

At our core, we all want to feel good, be accepted, and succeed. A critical issue in children's development is whether or not they experience unconditional positive regard from their primary caregivers. This feeling represents a confidence that one is a good person regardless of successes or failures, and that there's something inherently lovable

---

15. Sager, *Esquire.*

about each individual. From an outsider's perspective, it seems clear that Tiger Woods experienced more unconditional positive regard than Andre Agassi or Todd Marinovich. Tiger didn't seem to fight the same demons and endure the same battles that Todd did. That's not to say Tiger's life has been utopia, but rather he could center himself on the belief that he was good enough, whereas Todd and Andre appeared to doubt that. In fact, Tiger may have ended up on the other end of the spectrum where he felt untouchable, the center of the world, which can lead to narcissistic behavior of the sort we witnessed with his serial marital infidelity.

The subjective nature of conditional positive regard—when praise and approval follow only certain designated behaviors—means that it doesn't matter how successful you are, your belief system is built on the notion that "the only reason I'm worth something is if I succeed." Even during a success, an individual accustomed to conditional positive regard can feel used by family, friends, and society—all of whom they can perceive as caring only about success, not the person. Had Todd Marinovich known he was a great person regardless of his completion percentage, odds are he would have lasted longer in the NFL, and more important, he would have been happier and more fulfilled.

Throughout this chapter, we have focused on the ways that three prominent athletes' fathers were overinvolved in their careers. Marv Marinovich, Mike Agassi, and Earl Woods are certainly not the only parents to do so in the hopes of producing an elite athlete. Jennifer Capriati, Serena and Venus Williams, Sean O'Hair, and Michelle Wie have received attention for similar upbringings. It's worth noting the frequency with which we hear these stories about athletes from tennis or golf, the two most lucrative individual sports, which are also sports in which you don't need to be freakishly tall, strong, or fast to excel. It's as if parents who are controlling and overinvolved view individual sports as more controllable than team sports, and also consider sports with an easier physical access point to be better options than sports that require immense size, speed, and strength.

In his bestselling book, *Outliers*, Malcolm Gladwell highlights three factors that seem to predict success: talent, tremendous work ethic, and opportunity. Todd Marinovich, Andre Agassi, and Tiger Woods all achieved incredible success at a young age, and all three possessed talent, they worked incredibly hard, and their well-intentioned fathers provided them with unique opportunities to improve. Unfortunately, life isn't all about measureable success—as Marinovich's arrests and escape through drugs, Agassi's mental and physical pain, and Woods' marital infidelities demonstrate. When we invest all our energy in one outcome, success, other important markers of development and growth are often stunted.

Sadly, I don't expect the trend to change anytime soon. With so much money to be made in athletics, parents ignore the astronomical odds of their children attaining stardom as they envision grooming the next Todd, Andre, or Tiger. We may have hit a new low in August 2010 when *Sports Illustrated* did a feature story on five-year-old Ariel Antigua. Antigua is a baseball phenom whose YouTube videos have become Internet sensations. He's being heralded as a future major-league superstar. Why anyone, media or parents, would subject a five-year-old to those expectations is a mystery to me.

Of course, we must remember that most parents, even those profiled in this chapter, are well intentioned. Consider the sentiment captured by the following quote from a loving parent who would sacrifice anything for his child: "Some guys think the most important thing in life is their jobs, the stock market, whatever. To me, it was my kids. The question I asked myself was, 'How well could a kid develop if you provided him with the perfect environment?'"?[16]

What a testament to sacrifice and unconditional love. Who is the parent quoted above? None other than Marv Marinovich. The ultimate WOSP, Marv was extremely well intentioned, but even more overinvolved.

Words of Wisdom for WOSPs

1. Athletic excellence isn't the only measure of success for young athletes. Focus on the higher goals of sports as you evaluate your children's progress.

2. Allow your children the freedom to choose how invested they will be in activities they're passionate about. Provide opportunities and challenges for your children, but let their passion drive the extent of their involvement.

3. Too much pressure with any activity is dangerous, and a lack of balance in kids' lives will be costly at some point. Sports ought to be fun, and kids ought to have a choice in playing them. WOSPs' best intentions can go awry, so remember to step back and periodically check whether or not your children are deriving benefits, feeling pressure, or getting out of balance in their athletic activities.

---

16. Mike Sager, "Todd Marinovich: The Man Who Never Was," *Esquire*, March 2009, http://www.esquire.com/sports/a5720/todd-marinovich-0509.

5

The ARC of Success: How to Make Lemonade out of Lemons

The first day of summer basketball camp is marked with enthusiasm, excitement, and some nerves on the part of campers and coaches. Picture this scene: Monday morning, 8:30 a.m., and the gym opens. As the ten baskets are lowered, creaking into place, the lights flash on, illuminating one hundred youngsters, who hurriedly sprint their lunches over to the side wall so they can be first in line to grab a basketball. Although camp doesn't officially begin until 9:00 a.m., campers are bright-eyed and eager. You see the same scene over and over—a boy or girl, a ball, and a dream. It's fascinating to watch the initial interactions between the campers. Some campers know others already and quickly form groups. Other children grab a basketball and diligently begin working out, either uninterested in or uncomfortable with meeting others at this point. Whether nervous, anxious, or excited, the decibel level goes from silent to deafening in a few short minutes. The excitement is palpable as the campers survey the landscape on which the next week of their lives will play out. Invariably, on the fringes of camp, there will be a couple of campers who appear completely disinterested, sitting alone against a gym wall as if they're ready for camp to be over. Unfortunately for them, the week hasn't even begun yet.

Several years ago, one of those campers strolled through the doors of the University of St. Thomas Fieldhouse. A young boy came to camp in a dirty t-shirt, cutoff jean shorts, and filthy tennis shoes that were designed for skateboarding, not basketball. Willy (not his real name) was eleven years old, severely overweight, and his facial expression suggested he was headed for a root canal, not a basketball camp. He didn't move from the side wall until 9:00 a.m., when I blew the whistle three times to alert campers to congregate under the basket.

Ninety-nine players jogged over to where I was standing; one walked at a snail's pace. After taking nearly two minutes to travel fifty feet, Willy finally made it over to the rest of the group. While speaking to the camp, it was hard not to notice the complete lack of interest on Willy's face. He leaned back until he was lying down. Recognizing his attitude was going to be a problem, I asked him to sit up straight. When he didn't move, I asked him again, and he begrudgingly complied. I went through the rules at camp which all fall under the general principle of respect. I tell the campers that if they respect their teammates, opponents, coaches, and equipment (gym, basketballs, etc.), we'll have a good week full of hard work and fun. I went on to provide multiple examples of behaviors that demonstrate respect and those that don't.

We proceeded to stretch and warm up as one large group on the court. During warm-ups, the boy refused to move. He claimed first that he was already loose and then that he was injured. It was difficult to believe either claim because he hadn't really moved yet. We conclude warm-ups each day with one jumping jack. If everyone in camp does one jumping jack at the same time, no more and no less, we're done and we move on to the next drill. However, if anyone does zero or two jumping jacks, then we proceed to do two jumping jacks. Getting one hundred campers synchronized isn't always easy, so it's relatively common that a couple campers do a second jumping jack. This is typically followed by mild embarrassment and giggling when they hear we will now do two jumping jacks. If there's another mistake, we move up to four jumping jacks, and continue doubling the amount each time a camper is out of sync. Still, the campers think the process is pretty funny, until they realize on the series of eight jumping jacks that at the rate they're going, sixteen, thirty-two, and then sixty-four jumping jacks aren't far behind. Campers begin to figure out that it will behoove them to be precise in their jumping jacks. This relatively easy drill offers three major lessons to campers:

1. To be a successful team, everyone has to do their part. If a camper is struggling, rather than making fun of him, we encourage other campers to remind him of how many jumping jacks to do.

2. To be great at anything in life, you must be able to listen and concentrate. I tell campers that I have never worked with someone truly great who's a poor listener. To achieve excellence, you must learn; and to learn, you must listen and pay attention.

3. All campers would agree that this one jumping jack is

a simple task. However, it gets increasingly difficult to coordinate a hundred campers attempting thirty-two or sixty-four jumping jacks. The message to the campers is to master the simple things in life so they can move on to more difficult skills. Doing math is simple if you learn basic addition and subtraction, but if you don't master those skills, higher-level math is virtually impossible. In basketball, if you learn to make a left-handed lay-up, it's possible to begin working on more complex moves. However, if players don't learn to dribble or make lay-ups at a young age, working on advanced techniques is pointless. In the same vein, it's easy to do one jumping jack, but it's harder to do sixty-four, after fatigue has set in. We want campers to understand the value of doing simple things well time after time. As Aristotle wrote, "Excellence is not an act, but a habit."

As we began jumping jacks, it quickly became apparent that Willy had no interest in participating. He refused to do one jumping jack, then two, and then four. At this point, some campers who were standing nearby reminded him that the whole camp had to do the jumping jacks to move on to the next activity. By the time he refused to do sixteen jumping jacks, he was crying uncontrollably in the back row of campers, claiming that his knees and back hurt too much to do anything, swearing repeatedly to one of the coaches that, "I don't want to do this bull****." At this point, I wasn't pleased, because the first day of camp was having a less-than-stellar start thanks to Willy's antics. I pulled him aside and sat him down, and he continued to sob hysterically. I couldn't make out any of what he was saying because he was simultaneously crying and yelling. It was crystal clear he wanted to be anywhere but camp. He continued to curse, cry, and complain for the next five minutes. I told him I'd give him some time to settle down, and then we'd talk.

He calmed down a bit, and I laid out my expectations if he were to remain at camp. While doing so, it became apparent that he was hoping to be sent home. As I talked to him further, I was ready to call his mom and send him home, when something in his eyes told me he badly needed help. I was struck by how sad and angry Willy's eyes looked as he told me how much he hated basketball. As I talked to him, I asked myself if there was some way he could still learn a valuable lesson and maybe even enjoy his time at camp.

What Is Intrinsic Motivation?

Most campers are there because they want to be; others are forced to attend by a parent. Intrinsic motivation is the desire to participate in an activity for its own sake. This unique type of motivation defines the type of passionate involvement that is marked by enjoyment. Intrinsically motivated activities are uncontaminated by the lure of money, rewards, or prestige—which are all extrinsic motivators. One can think of any action on a two-dimensional matrix, where one could be high or low on both extrinsic and intrinsic motivation. From a theoretical perspective, it is difficult to perfectly measure intrinsic motivation. Most researchers measure intrinsic motivation in three ways—through observation of free-choice behavior; through self-reported measures of enjoyment; and through measures of behavioral intention, where participants report what they intend to do in the future.

None of these measures is perfect, and a psychologist (or a

philosopher) could spend a career attempting to prove that pure intrinsic motivation exists. For purposes of this discussion, consider intrinsically motivated activities as those that you would engage in on a Saturday afternoon when you have no obligations—no work, no chores, no assignments, no appointments. What would you choose to do? The answers to this question typically reveal activities that we're intrinsically motivated to take part in because we enjoy them. When I pose this question to my students, they often identify activities such as reading, biking, playing the guitar, running, singing, dancing, playing sports, and spending time with friends. While the responses vary widely, there's a fascinating overlap in their explanations for *why* that activity is intrinsically motivating.

The ARC of Success: Self-Determination Theory

In explaining their activity choices for a free Saturday afternoon, the most frequently cited reason is *fun*. While not inaccurate, this explanation is a bit superficial, as we discussed in Chapter 3. It requires additional layers of analysis to understand what makes an activity enjoyable. Students typically report that when engaged in their chosen activities, they (1) feel little pressure and have free choice to perform the activity, (2) experience rewarding interactions with friends, family, teammates, and colleagues, and (3) possess a moderate to high degree of skill in the activity. These three categories of explanations tie nicely into self-determination theory (SDT), a theory designed to understand people's choices in varied fields of human behavior. SDT is based on the premise that humans are driven to grow and flourish, and that our personalities and social environments play major roles in determining the extent to which we feel these growth needs are met. Numerous studies have been published documenting the powerful role of three factors in determining our experience within an activity:

1. *Autonomy*: the extent to which one freely chooses to engage in an activity.

2. *Relatedness*: the extent to which one fosters positive relationships with others.

3. *Competence*: the extent to which one possesses skill.

These basic human needs provide a useful framework through which we can understand the presence or absence of intrinsic motivation.

The Absence of ARC (Autonomy, Relatedness, Competence)

As the morning went on, Willy begrudgingly took part in drills, but only when they didn't require much physical exertion on his part. Shooting drills he tolerated; defensive drills that required him to stay in an athletic stance for forty-five seconds he did not. Willy showed some improvement in his attitude, but still caused periodic disruptions and required more attention than any other camper. We took a break for lunch at noon. Willy quickly wolfed down his lunch and sauntered over to a group of five campers. He asked them if they'd like to play a shooting game called Lightning. This is a popular game among campers. In the game, players form a line with the first two players in line each holding a basketball. Each player tries to make a shot before the person in line in front of him, and the person behind him does the same thing. Once you make a basket, you pass the ball back to the next person in line. The game continues until only one player is left standing.

I was pleased and mildly shocked that Willy went out of his way to initiate a game with others, particularly after his actions earlier in the day had alienated many of the other campers. This was progress for Willy. He'd made an effort and made himself vulnerable to others. I was eager to see how the other campers would respond. Unfortunately, the other campers were still finishing their lunches and told Willy they weren't interested in playing.

Willy didn't seem too upset and asked me for permission to leave the gym to use the restroom. I felt great, thinking we'd made some real progress with Willy in only a couple hours. That all changed quickly. Three minutes later, he walked back through the gym doors and saw the same group of campers he had just asked to play Lightning. They had finished their lunches and lo and behold, what were they doing? Playing a game of Lightning. Willy was only two steps into the gymnasium when he saw them. Willy's face was bright red, with eyes that showed a blend of rage and horror, as if he felt the other campers had plotted to start the game once he left the gym (which was not the case). He stared for a moment before screaming, "This is so F*****D UUUUUUUUUPP!"

The echo throughout the cavernous gym stopped all one hundred boys in their tracks. Willy was crying now, and had turned around to run out of the gym. The other campers were silent, unsure of what had just happened. Even the boys playing Lightning were confused, because they started the game when Willy wasn't present. A couple coaches ran after Willy, trying to find him to calm him down. After several minutes of searching for Willy, they returned to the gym. I told them to continue looking until they found him. They finally did find him—in a bathroom, with a mop on his head, hiding inside a garbage can. Willy wouldn't move, and he was so emotional he was incoherent. When they finally convinced Willy to come out of the garbage can, he took off running again, this time out of the athletic complex and into the main quadrangle of the university. After several more minutes, the coaches found him, this time hiding underneath a bench near the flagpole. He wouldn't move. He wouldn't talk. Finally, after ten minutes, he stood up and walked back to the gym with the coaches.

Willy sat out the rest of that day's activities. Immediately after camp, I called his mother. I told her what Willy had done, but that something told me not to kick him out of camp and send him home. I tried to be understanding, while also conveying the seriousness of Willy's actions.

His mother was quiet for several seconds and then sighed the sigh of a mother who has tried everything to no avail. "Willy's father and I are divorced, and he's been in and out of prison for some time. Whenever his dad is around Willy, he talks negatively about both himself and Willy." I asked her why Willy came to camp. She said some of his classmates were attending, although none of them were friends with Willy.

How can we understand Willy's behavior, particularly when the majority of the incidents that set him off that day (warm-ups, jumping jacks, and a shooting game at lunch) were seemingly minor? Consider self-determination theory, and how Willy would score on measures of autonomy, relatedness, and competence. Was he autonomous? Did he freely choose to attend camp? No, his mother signed him up, even though he had little interest in basketball, and still less interest in physical exertion of any kind. Was there relatedness? Did he have others at camp with whom he could share a positive experience? No, he knew very few kids at camp, and the ones he knew from his school weren't his friends. Rather, they often battled with him at school, and camp was one more place for negative interactions to take place. In addition, Willy wasn't inclined to initiate conversations with others in an attempt to make new friends. Was he competent? No, he was inexperienced at basketball, not very athletic, and not in good shape.

Combine the absence of autonomy, relatedness, and competence for Willy and we have a young boy who was signed up for camp by his well-intentioned mother even though he had little interest in attending a camp where he knew few kids, didn't get along well with the ones he did know, and was playing a sport in which he didn't possess much skill. This trifecta is a perfect recipe for a complete and utter lack of intrinsic motivation. As Willy's mom and I concluded our conversation, I was impressed with both her honesty and her hope that we would accept him back at camp the next morning. I told her we would, but that any more outbursts or unruly behavior would force me to send Willy home.

As parents, we can learn a great deal from Willy's story. In order for our children to be passionate about what they're doing, we should aim to provide them with environments that facilitate autonomy, relatedness, and competence. These qualities can't be deposited in kids like money in a bank; they have to be developed over time. To the extent that we provide our children with choices, help facilitate the development of healthy relationships, and provide them opportunities to become more competent, we'll see them become more intrinsically motivated.

Contrast this approach that relies on supporting our children's autonomy with Marv Marinovich's control over virtually every aspect of his son Todd's schedule and his limited interactions with others. Even though Todd was incredibly competent, at some point the absence of autonomy and relatedness caught up with him. Sometimes parents' good intentions manifest in controlling efforts to push children past the point they want to go. It's one thing if a child yearns to be great and is driven to be the best. However, if a parent tries to force a dream onto a child, then that dream will always be the parent's, not the child's. Of autonomy, relatedness, and competence, autonomy is where parents' best intentions usually go astray. Why? Because as parents we believe we know what's best (and in many cases we may be right), but imposing our beliefs and goals on others is often dangerous.

Autonomy Is Key

My high school baseball coach, Dennis Denning, is a legend in the Midwest. Dennis had played several years of professional ball, ascending to Baltimore's Triple-A team before an injury ended his career. (The injury happened while Dennis was working at a playground; he was hurt playing baseball with a young player who went on to make the Baseball Hall of Fame, Paul Molitor). As a high school coach, Denning's teams won six Minnesota state baseball championships in a twelve-year span (1981, 1982, 1986, 1989, 1990, and 1992), an astounding accomplishment—particularly in baseball, where a star pitcher can end an opponent's season with one dominating performance. In 1994, Denning moved on to the University of St. Thomas, where he took over a previously average baseball program. Over the next fifteen years, his teams won more than 77 percent of their games, the highest winning percentage of any Division III baseball coach in the country during that time. In 1999 and 2000, his teams were second in the nation in Division III baseball, and in 2001 and 2009, his team won the D-III national championship.

Dennis's son, Wes, and I are the same age, and we became close friends in grade school while attending Coach Denning's baseball camps. As the son of a coach known everywhere in the state of Minnesota, Wes had high expectations surrounding his baseball career. In grade school, Wes was very fast, but not big or strong. He was a good baseball player, fundamentally sound, but he didn't stand out on the diamond. I recall people asking Coach Denning when he was going to start pushing Wes to be great. His response was always the same, and it struck my twelve-year-old self as incredibly sensible and thoughtful. "I've let Wes know that if he decides he wants to try to be great at baseball, I'll help him in any way I can. Until then, I'm staying away from coaching him, pushing him, or controlling him."

Whatever happened to Wes's career? He blossomed in high school, and became as passionate about baseball as anyone I've ever seen. He was a tireless worker and an All-State player who eventually received a scholarship to the University of Minnesota, where he had an outstanding career. He was drafted by the Montreal Expos and played several years in their minor-league system. I'm convinced Wes would've never attained such success, nor would they have had such a strong father-son relationship, had Coach Denning pressured Wes to devote more time to baseball as a youngster. The coach's refreshing attitude highlights the value of providing a child with autonomy to promote intrinsic motivation. Less truly can be more when it comes to youth sports and motivation.

Todd and Andre: Holes in the ARC

Returning to the analysis of Todd Marinovich, Andre Agassi, and Tiger Woods—it's clear that all three athletes were supremely competent. Their excellence was likely due in part to the extreme involvement of their fathers. Clearly, parental involvement can provide a foundation of skills that can serve a young athlete well for years to come. So if all three boys were already on the national radar screen as youngsters, why did they experience such different outcomes?

In terms of competence, all three boys were outstanding. However, it appears that Marinovich and Agassi both doubted their competence, because nothing they did could ever meet their fathers' expectations. When Agassi won the 1992 Wimbledon Championship at age twenty-two, he was elated. According to the description in his autobiography, *Open*, he finally felt the unadulterated joy he thought championships might bring him. When he called his father, the first thing his dad did was to admonish him for losing the fourth set. When Agassi responded that it was good he bounced back and won the fifth set, he heard no response. After several seconds, Andre realized his dad couldn't speak because he was crying. At the pinnacle of his son's career, on a day when he should have been rejoicing that their hard work had paid off, Mike Agassi was in tears, and unable to compliment his son (164–5).

When it comes to relatedness, none of the three had overly social childhoods. This was probably less detrimental to Woods's and Agassi's careers because they pursued sports that are entirely individual. An internal focus may work better in golf or tennis compared to football, particularly since Marinovich was a quarterback—arguably the most important role on the field. The position requires the ability to communicate strategy, provide feedback, and create a vision among the entire offense. Marinovich's focus on his own development may have precluded him from developing the people skills so essential to a quarterback's leadership. In any case, stronger peer relationships would likely have benefitted Marinovich, Agassi, and Woods. In his autobiography, Agassi wrote that at age ten he was playing soccer, and wished he could play that instead of tennis because he wanted teammates and less pressure. At one point his father became so enraged that Andre was playing soccer that he stormed onto the field and told the coach to take his son out of the game. Mike Agassi took Andre's uniform and threw it at the coach. Andre pleaded with his father, telling him he would rather be on a team, to which his dad screamed, "You're a tennis player! You're going to be number one in the world! You're going to make lots of money. That's the plan and that's the end of it" (57). How ironic that Andre did all those things, and it probably never brought him the same joy he would've gotten from being part of a successful soccer team.

When we examine autonomy, we begin to see the biggest differences between the way Tiger Woods was raised compared to Todd Marinovich and Andre Agassi. Todd and Andre had their days, weeks, and years scripted. Tiger was given a choice (at least he perceived it that way). As a result, Tiger grew up feeling the choice to play golf was his, whereas Todd and Andre felt coerced, as if they had no choice. The long-term ramifications for intrinsic motivation are enormous, which likely explains why Marinovich and Agassi rebelled, while Tiger maintained his passion for the game, even through the ups and downs in his career.

What to Do with Willy?

Unfortunately, Willy didn't attend camp of his own volition, and there was nothing we could do in the short term to address his lack of autonomy. Furthermore, there would be no quick fix to turn Willy into a competent basketball player. So, with autonomy and competence out of the equation, we decided to work on the relatedness part of the ARC to success. When Willy arrived on Tuesday morning, he looked even less excited than the day before. I greeted him and his mom and asked if I could speak with him one on one. I told him how proud I was that he'd decided to return (my attempt to promote feelings of autonomy in Willy), and that I expected him to behave well the rest of the week (trying to instill accountability and the belief that I thought he could do it). I also let Willy know that if he had any problems, he should see the specific coach working with his age group, and if that coach couldn't help him, he should come find me. I also alerted the coaches to Willy's plight, and encouraged them to keep a special eye out for times when Willy worked hard so that they could offer legitimate positive feedback.

Over the course of the second day, Willy was much better, listening well, causing no major disruptions, and showing a decent effort periodically. He was still below average in talent, but he started to see that working hard brought him positive recognition from both his coaches and his teammates. In addition, he stopped himself before getting into an altercation with an opponent over what Willy perceived was rough play. All in all, the day was a huge success, in large part due to the connection Willy began to feel with both coaches and campers. In Willy's case, relatedness was the best bet to nurture his intrinsic motivation. We need to tailor our approach to fostering that powerful internal drive to the individual needs of each young athlete.

The Extrinsic-Intrinsic Motivation Continuum

Intrinsic motivation comes naturally when children experience autonomy, relatedness, and competence. However, when some or all of these are absent, it's exceedingly difficult for a child to develop intrinsic motivation. In those cases, it may be necessary to utilize an extrinsic motivator to get a young athlete like Willy started. If Willy is unwilling to do jumping jacks and we explain that refusing to do drills results in extra running, Willy may now be sufficiently motivated to jump. Essentially, we can use the carrot-or-stick approach to extrinsically motivate children who lack intrinsic motivation. For activities that children find boring, the use of rewards or some other external control may be necessary. These rewards don't come without risks, which I'll discuss in the next chapter. Used excessively, rewards can stifle the very motivation they're intended to create and maintain. Used appropriately, however, rewards can help encourage behaviors that are important for children to learn.

The Power of Skittles

Take toilet training. My older son Jack was nearly three years old and hadn't yet shown any interest in toilet training. He was in no way intrinsically motivated to use the toilet. Many experts encourage removing a child's diaper and letting him wet himself. The idea is that sooner or later, the child will grow tired of being wet and smelly and begin using the toilet. However, depending on a family's schedule, allowing a child to wallow in urine may not be the first choice for toilet training. One night, as an experiment (my poor boys), I offered

Jack a Skittle if he used the toilet to urinate, and three Skittles if he used it for number two. We were eating dinner when Jack got up and announced he had to go number two. I smiled, knowing how badly he wanted Skittles, but also recalling how little interest he'd shown in the toilet. Thirty seconds later Jack shouted, "I did it mineself. I did it mineself. I pooped in the toilet! I get four Skittles!" (He had also urinated—clearly his math skills were ahead of his verbal skills.) He returned to the kitchen, ate his Skittles, and three minutes later got up and announced he had to go to the bathroom again. I tried to explain that one can't summon a bowel movement at the drop of a hat, but he was already grunting and groaning in the bathroom. My laughter was interrupted by Jack's cry, "I did it again. I pooped again!" I checked on him and sure enough, he had earned three more Skittles. We sat down to finish dinner when two minutes later he got up without a word and headed for the bathroom again. This time, I just listened as he engaged in thirty seconds of prolonged grunting. I was in near hysterics when he exclaimed, "I pooped AGAIN. Three more Skittles." My excitement over his toilet training was tempered by the fact that the bag of Skittles was half gone in a matter of minutes. (OK, maybe I had a few as well.) Amazingly, from that point on, Jack used the toilet whenever he had to go to the bathroom. Clearly, the promise of a reward had motivated him to do something he wouldn't otherwise have tried.

Not only was the reward effective for Jack, but the story also illustrates that sometimes an external reward can elicit a behavior that a child knows how to do, but isn't sufficiently motivated to accomplish. I suppose we could have waited for Jack to begin preschool and then the embarrassment of wetting his pants in front of his classmates would've been sufficient to motivate him to become toilet trained. However, there are times when it's important to produce a behavior that a child is capable of performing, but that doesn't provide motivation on its own. In these cases, rewards may help do the trick.

Of course, it would be dangerous if Jack became addicted to Skittles (did I mention they're still his candy of choice?), so weaning a child off of a reward is important. This is where parents can work to move the child from the external end of the motivational continuum to the internal end. How does this happen? As the child begins to engage in an activity, parents can work to shift the focus away from the reward and onto the activity. Commenting on how well the child is doing (competence) and how nice it is for the child to be independent (autonomy) are both examples of how to move children from the extrinsic end of the continuum to the intrinsic side.

Carol Sansone is a psychology professor at the University of Utah who has studied the many ways people are able to take dull activities and make them enjoyable. Typically, this starts by creating some sort of external goal that takes the focus off the boring activity. Over time, Sansone has observed, as individuals become better and better at a task, they may actually come to enjoy it, shifting their motivation from extrinsic to intrinsic.[17]

Whatever Happened to Willy?

The rest of the week at basketball camp went much better for Willy. Each day there were times he became frustrated, typically because he lacked the stamina to physically perform the way he wanted. It would be up to him to decide if he wanted to become more competent. We tried to

---

17. Carol Sansone, Charlene Weir, Lora Harpster, and Carolyn Morgan. "Once a boring task always a boring task?: Interest as a self-regulatory mechanism," *Journal of Personality and Social Psychology* 63 (1992), 379–90.

create feelings of relatedness for Willy and it seemed to work. By the end of the week, he had developed trust in a couple of the coaches and even talked about coming back for another camp. It was heartwarming to see how proud he was to have made it through the entire week of camp when he'd been ready to quit five minutes into the first day.

Willy returned to camp the next summer, and immediately set out to reconnect with the coaches he'd met the previous year. It was hard to believe this was the same child who had single-handedly disrupted an entire camp. Willy had used relatedness to form trust, and this allowed him to improve to the point where he freely chose to attend more camps.

Later that summer Willy signed up for an offensive-skills camp, which differs from the camps he'd already attended in its structure and the types of drills. During this camp, he quickly reverted back to causing problems, and he came to us at lunch to complain that camp was boring and he wanted to go home. We spent considerable time explaining why we did different drills and reminded him that he'd chosen to attend this camp (autonomy), that his teammates were counting on him (relatedness), and that these drills would help him become a better player (competence). He agreed to work at it, and Willy ended up returning to a variety of our camps for the next five years, until he was too old to attend. This was one of the best success stories I've seen at camp—it was proof in action that all children are capable of learning valuable lessons through sports.

A few years later, I was in a local high school recruiting a student athlete when I heard a voice call out, "Coach Tauer!" I looked over and there was Willy with a huge grin on his face. Willy would never be a professional athlete, but he did go on to play football in high school. I asked him if he remembered that first day of camp and with a sheepish grin he simply said, "I've grown up a bit since then,

Coach." By supporting their children, but not allowing them the easy way out, parents like Willy's mom do their children a tremendous service. Along his sometimes difficult journey, Willy was able to develop feelings of autonomy, relatedness, and competence that were useful on and off the court. Each of us has the ability to make a difference in our children's lives by providing them the tools and opportunities to feel autonomy, relatedness, and competence.

Words of Wisdom for WOSPs

1. Check the ARC to success. Ask yourself if your children are feeling autonomy, relatedness, and competence. Are you promoting the ARC? Are you giving them choices? Do they have opportunities to interact with other children? Do they feel good about their skills? Are you complimenting them when they deserve it?

2. If your child needs a kick-start of motivation, consider using extrinsic motivators. Although dangerous if overused— and generally not necessary when someone is already intrinsically motivated—extrinsic motivators can help get your child energized and excited about a task or challenge.

3. Intrinsic motivation is important when it comes to youth sports. Asking your children what they enjoy, what they learn, and what they can improve on in youth sports is a vital way to help them understand and appreciate the progress they've made and the future growth they can anticipate.

6

Turning Lemonade into Sour Lemons

Latrell Sprewell grew up in Milwaukee, Wisconsin, where he attended Washington High School, an inner-city public school. After going to junior college in Missouri, Sprewell played for the University of Alabama for two seasons before being selected in the first round of the NBA draft by the Golden State Warriors. Sprewell went on to have a thirteen-year career, was a four-time NBA All-Star, scored more than sixteen thousand career points, and was noted for being one of the best all-around players in the world for several years. He was tenacious, aggressive, and a fiery competitor. However, when most sports fans think of Sprewell, they likely first remember two incidents unrelated to his athletic achievements.

At a Golden State Warriors practice in 1997, he became angered and frustrated, and tried to choke his head coach, P. J. Carlesimo. Immediately, Sprewell became the poster boy for everything wrong with professional sports. He was suspended by the NBA for the remainder of the season, and a little more than a year later he was traded to the New York Knicks. His career was at an uncertain crossroads, yet he helped lead the Knicks to the 1999 NBA Finals, where they were defeated by the San Antonio Spurs. Fans appeared very willing to forgive him, provided that he played well. His story is another example in a long line that demonstrates how quickly people forgive bad behavior as long as an athlete's performance doesn't suffer.

The second incident that many sports fans recall came during Sprewell's stint with the Minnesota Timberwolves. The 2003–04 season was his first with Minnesota. Along with Kevin Garnett and Sam Cassell, Sprewell was part of the highest-scoring trio in the NBA. In their fifteenth year as a much-maligned franchise, the Timberwolves experienced unprecedented success. They reached the Western Conference Finals before losing a hard-fought series with the Los Angeles Lakers. The Timberwolves had never won a playoff series before 2004 and they haven't won one since. Fans loved Sprewell's hard-nosed play and fiery competitiveness. His next season with Minnesota wasn't nearly as good, with Sprewell posting the lowest scoring average of his career.

Sprewell's contract, which had paid him more than $14 million per season, expired at the conclusion of 2003–04 season. In the process of negotiating a new contract, the Timberwolves offered him a three-year, $21 million contract. Sprewell was outraged, responding infamously, "I've got my family to feed." This single comment outraged fans—understandably so—and it will live in infamy as an exemplar of the attitudes of spoiled professional athletes. How did we get to a point where a man who grew up in a rough neighborhood in

Milwaukee, fought valiantly on the court, moved through junior college to the University of Alabama, and then on to the NBA believed that $21 million for three years of playing a *game* was beneath him and an insufficient amount to provide for his family? How does the pure intrinsic motivation so many children display for sports at a young age get undermined along the way? How do the same children who grew up in New York City shoveling snow off the playground just so they could shoot hoops, or those who fashioned baseballs out of socks and used broom handles for bats, turn into adults who refuse to play for millions and millions of dollars?

In the previous chapter, I discussed practical ways parents can create environments conducive to intrinsic motivation. These strategies included ways to increase children's perceptions of their own autonomy, relatedness, and competence. While it's quite challenging to create intrinsic motivation in a child who doesn't like an activity, it's frighteningly easy for parents to squelch intrinsic motivation in children who already possess it. In this chapter, I'll explore the myriad ways that parental overinvolvement can be detrimental to children's athletic experience and crush their existing intrinsic motivation.

Interest and Pressure

Parental involvement may come in many forms, ranging from encouragement or subtle pressure to more controlling behaviors involving rewards and punishment. To understand the combined effects of children's interest and parental involvement, it may be helpful to consider the following two-by-two matrix:

Parental Pressure and/or Involvement

Low   **High**

Child's Interest

Low	Cognitive Dissonance	Extrinsic Motivation
High	Intrinsic Motivation	Overjustification Effect

Cognitive Dissonance

Picture a child who doesn't particularly enjoy volleyball. Her parents don't pressure her to play, yet she's on the team and practices hard every day. In the upper-left quadrant, we see cognitive dissonance, which is an uncomfortable psychological tension due to conflicting attitudes and behaviors. Children who engage in an activity they don't enjoy and that they aren't pressured to do may experience cognitive dissonance. Often, dissonance leads us to justify our efforts and behaviors by changing our attitudes. In the example above, the girl would likely search for reasons to justify all the time and energy she spent playing volleyball. In the mid-twentieth century, cognitive dissonance theory became one of the dominant theories in the field of social psychology. It provides a framework for understanding how people think and act when they experience conflict between their attitudes and behavior.

Extrinsic Motivation

Now picture the nine-year-old boy who attended my camp this summer, had no interest in basketball, and refused to work hard in any of the drills. When one of the coaches asked the boy why he was attending camp if he didn't enjoy basketball, the boy responded that he was being paid ten dollars per day to attend camp! In the upper-right quadrant, we see this represented by extrinsic motivation. In this case, the boy had no real desire to attend camp other than as a means to an end—i.e., money. While this extrinsically motivated behavior isn't desirable, some would argue that it's a start, particularly in the case of activities or behaviors that children ought to do for their own good. In other words, rewarding a child in this case is unlikely to dampen the little interest he has in the activity.

Intrinsic Motivation

Of course, we'd all prefer that children take part in an activity because they're interested in it, depicted in the lower-left quadrant. Here, we find children who participate in sports purely because they love to play, not because of any parental pressure. Take Howie Long, the Hall of Fame football star who, in the role of defensive end, led the Oakland Raiders to the 1983 Super Bowl Championship. Playing at the University of Virginia in 2007, his son Chris was the top defensive lineman in the nation, and now Chris plays for the St. Louis Rams. One imagines this overlap of experience would be a recipe for overinvolvement—a parent who has had success and possesses unmatched expertise in the sport and position his son now plays. However, Howie

Long took a hands-off approach, dating back to the days of his own NFL career. "My wife and I have the same philosophy. The comparison and story line is always there and it's a convenient hook for people, which I understand. But I do as much as I possibly can to make sure that Chris has the opportunity to be his own man and enjoy his college experience as both a student and athlete."[18]

While at Virginia, Chris's dad lived only a few miles from where his son was the star, yet he stayed away for the most part, providing advice only when his son asked for it. He attended only home games, and let his son learn and develop naturally, even when the coaches encouraged Howie to come around more often. Head coach Al Groh said, "I told Howie, 'Come on around, don't let that keep you away.' I even mentioned to Chris one time, 'Your dad, he's trying to give you your own space, bud. Tell him it's OK.'"[19]

Autonomy, relatedness, and competence lead to intrinsic motivation, and Howie Long created an environment that facilitated all of these for his son Chris. Thus, it's no surprise that Chris possesses high levels of intrinsic motivation.

Overjustification Effect

In the lower-right quadrant we see a case in which an athlete possesses a high level of interest and also experiences pressure in the form of rewards, money, parental pressure or some other outside force.

---

18. Mark Schlabach, "Howie Long Gives Son Chris the Room to Grow as a Player," espn.com, November 9, 2007, http://sports.espn.go.com/ncf/columns/story?id=3100700.
19. Schlabach, espn.com.

When I ask my students about this combination—getting paid to do something they love—their first response for the correct phrase to place in this box is "a dream." Instead, we often see this convergence lead to the overjustification effect, which as its name implies, occurs when one has too much justification for a behavior.

In a classic demonstration of the overjustification effect, Mark Lepper and his colleagues at Stanford University had five- to six-year-old children draw pictures with Magic Markers, an activity they all found interesting, based on their past behavior. The purpose of the experiment was to examine how rewards affect intrinsic motivation. One group of children was told that if they drew with the markers they'd receive a good-player award that would be placed on the wall for other children to see. The children were clearly excited by this prospect and they all drew with the markers. In a second group, children were merely asked to draw with the Magic Markers. Once again, all of the children complied. Then, over the next four days during the children's free-choice time, experimenters provided several opportunities in which they could choose to play with a variety of toys; among them were the Magic Markers. This is a commonly used behavioral measure of intrinsic motivation because it provides a glimpse at what the children choose to do when no one applies any pressure on them. Researchers were unobtrusively observing the children through a one-way mirror at the preschool.

When I ask students who is more likely to return to the Magic Markers, their typical response is the group that was rewarded because rewards bolster motivation. Counterintuitively, the group that wasn't rewarded spent twice as much time drawing with the markers over the next four days compared to the group that was rewarded. The researchers' explanation for this overjustification effect is that the children who weren't rewarded during the study had no problem identifying why they drew with the Magic Markers: they enjoyed drawing with them. The participants in the group that was rewarded, however, had a bit of a dilemma in understanding their behavior. Did they draw with the markers because they enjoyed doing so or because they received a reward? What changed for those children who were rewarded?

It appears that the way they thought about the activity *while* engaging in it was different when they were promised a reward. Am I drawing with the markers because I enjoy them, or because I will receive a reward? These children now had two explanations for their behavior, and at least some of them attributed this behavior to the reward. This is a classic case of the overjustification effect that illustrates how rewards can undermine children's existing interest in an activity. The children who weren't promised a reward had no problem identifying why they were drawing with the markers. However, the children who did receive a reward focused their attention on the reward, not the activity, and this affected their subsequent motivation. The implications of this finding are nearly limitless in youth sports, particularly given the pervasiveness of external pressure from parents, rewards, and competition. Although much of the experimental research on pressure and external controls has been conducted on rewards, there are clear parallels between the external pressure of rewards and the pressure that parents often place on their children to perform well in youth sports.

Applying the Overjustification Effect to Athletics

Professional athletes weren't compensated for playing sports in middle school, high school, or college (at least not legally). The overjustification effect helps us understand professional athletes' apparent shift in focus to money and prestige. Quite simply, when someone already loves what he or she is doing, it's dangerous to add a reward for the behavior because it can shift the focus from intrinsic to extrinsic. This is why we see athletes such as Latrell Sprewell, who have played for the love of the game, change their tune once they're highly compensated—claiming, for example, that a three-year, $20 million contract isn't sufficient enough to justify him playing basketball.

Bill Russell, the Hall of Fame Boston Celtics center said, "I remember that the game lost some of its magical qualities for me once I thought seriously about playing for a living. . . Whenever I walked on the court I began to calculate how this particular game might affect my future. Thoughts of money and prestige crept into my head. Over the years the professional game would turn more and more into a business."[20]

Even for young athletes who don't receive money, rewards can lead to the overjustification effect. This is one reason that in the sixteen years of my summer basketball camp, I've never awarded trophies for teams that win games or players who win contests. The self-esteem movement has led our culture to buy into the "everyone deserves a trophy" mindset. Extrinsic rewards can hamper intrinsic motivation. In the same way young children drawing with Magic Markers can have their focus shifted from intrinsic to extrinsic, and pro athletes can have their focus shifted from love of the sport to dollar signs, young athletes can worry more about receiving a trophy than how they're playing and what they're learning.

My dad always told me not to worry about trophies. He coached youth basketball for twenty-five years and never gave out trophies. "If there is a clear most valuable player," he said, "everybody already knows who it is. If it's unclear who the MVP is and there are several

---

20. James W. Johnson, *The Dandy Dons*. University of Nebraska Press, 2009, 158.

candidates, that award just causes hard feelings." My dad's reasoning always made sense to me—kids should be playing for the love of the game, not for a trophy or award.

Rewards in Action

Although I don't give trophies at my camps, two years ago a good friend who is in sales gave us several pairs of Billy Bob Teeth. At the time, these teeth were popular among teens as a gag gift. He suggested I give them out to the kids at camp who shot the best in the daily contest. Not even thinking about these as a reward, I gave out six pairs of teeth to the highest scorers in the daily free-throw contest. We moved on to our next activity, which was full-court games. What followed astounded me. Without fail, before each game the rest of the day, campers asked coaches if they would get Billy Bob Teeth if their team won. Not once during camp had they asked about a prize for winning, and now, after offering one set of rewards for shooting free throws, the majority of the campers had become preoccupied with what they might receive for winning a game. This was an unfortunate outcome. Most parents would agree that we'd much rather our children focus on the activity, or even on winning, as opposed to what type of reward they could earn with a victory. We spent several minutes at the end of that day of camp talking about the difference between intrinsic and extrinsic motivation to help the campers see the dangers of rewards when received for doing something we already enjoy.

In addition to undermining intrinsic motivation, there is a second problem with how rewards are frequently administered in our culture. In an "everybody deserves a reward" culture, rewards can render meaningless the feedback that young athletes rely upon to gauge their competence. Earlier we discussed the competing motives of feeling good versus being good. When everyone gets a trophy regardless of his or her performance, the need to feel good has trumped the need to be good. How does a child know if she performed well if everyone gets a trophy? One of the motivational benefits provided by feedback is that it can provide valuable information to help athletes develop a gauge to interpret excellent, good, average, and subpar performance. If everyone gets a trophy, athletes receive no useful feedback, and their attention is shifted to the extrinsic reward of receiving a trophy.

When my son Jack was two, we went to Hawaii. During our stay, he met several young girls who became his fast friends. He became pen pals with one of the girls and they kept in touch over the next couple years. He would tell me what to write: something along the lines of, "I had a birthday party. I got lots of presents. I am three years old." Then his friend Hannah from California would write back. In one update, she described her soccer season succinctly with this summary: "School is good. I am swimming a lot. I'm also playing soccer. Unforchanately [sic] we haven't won any games but I have gotten six trophies!"

I couldn't help but wonder how a six-year-old soccer player could have earned six trophies, regardless of how many wins the team had, much less receive six trophies without winning a game! Last year, on the final day of basketball camp, I explained to parents why I don't award trophies. This wasn't a planned speech, nor was it an extensive soliloquy on the empirical evidence surrounding rewards and intrinsic motivation. Rather, I simply explained to parents that I don't give rewards to children at camp because I want their focus to be on the game of basketball, not striving to get another trophy. As I was concluding my remarks, the entire crowd broke out into applause.

I was stunned. My intent hadn't been to impress anyone, but rather to give parents a warning that Jimmy and Jenny wouldn't be bringing home any hardware from camp. I had a line of parents after camp, each wanting to commend me for the focus on developing passion for the right reasons. I was flattered, but also puzzled. If parents are seemingly against trophies, then who is purchasing all these trophies for young athletes, and why?

The Parable of Ausubel

One of my favorite stories about the danger of rewards is known as the parable of Ausubel. Picture an elderly man who takes tremendous pride in his meticulously groomed yard. Ausubel becomes enraged when anyone steps foot on his lawn. Of course, this leads neighborhood children to perceive a challenge, and soon Ausubel's yard becomes the site of the daily after-school football game. Each day, the children would engage in a spirited game of football and Ausubel would quickly come out of his house, ranting and raving that they'd better get off his lawn immediately. The children would scatter temporarily, but return later, testing Ausubel's patience time after time. This went on for weeks, and Ausubel's pristine lawn was developing some rough patches.

At this point, Ausubel was at his wit's end and decided to try a different tactic. The next Monday, he greeted the kids on the sidewalk and said with a smile, "Thanks for coming by today, guys. If you'll play on my lawn today, I'll give each of you a quarter." The children, dumbfounded, smiled as they contemplated whether this qualified them as professional athletes. Each day that week, the boys showed up, played spirited games of football, and received a quarter apiece. The next Monday, Ausubel welcomed the boys back and told them they'd each receive ten cents per day. Smiling, they thanked him and went about their business. The third week, Ausubel paid them a nickel each per day, and when they showed up the fourth Monday, there was a little less bounce in their steps. When Ausubel told them that he'd only be able to pay them one penny each, they looked at each other and one replied, "If you think we're gonna play on your lousy lawn for a penny, you're nuts!" The boys picked up their football, walked off, and never returned.

Ausubel had effectively applied the principle of the overjustification effect to decrease the intrinsic motivation the boys had for playing football in his yard. While most of the time we want to maximize motivation, there are times when being able to dampen it is beneficial. Recently, my two sons Jack and Adam were making lots of noise at the dinner table. They were bouncing off the walls, and I decided to try an experiment. Rather than asking them to be quiet and stifling their enthusiasm, I told them I wanted to see who could make the most noise. First Jack screamed, then Adam. Back and forth they went. After they were done, I gave them each a Starburst for making so much noise. They calmed down, ate their dinner, and the night proceeded smoothly. Who would've thought the overjustification effect could get children to behave so easily?

Complexity of Rewards

Regardless of one's stance on rewards, they are ubiquitous in our society. They take the form of bonuses in the workplace, trophies for athletics, and prizes for schoolchildren as a reward for reading books—to name just a few examples. Consider the BOOK IT! reading program. In many schools, if children read a certain number of books, they receive a prize, often in the form of a pizza party. Some have remarked that it seems odd to reward children with something unhealthy, as if to imply that if you'll appease us by reading books, we'll let you eat whatever you want. A better suggestion, according to Alfie Kohn, author of *Punished by Rewards* (1999), would be to reward children for reading books by providing them with more books. In other words, reward a desired behavior with a chance to continue engaging in the desired behavior.

Over the past several decades, the effect of rewards on motivation has been a hot topic in the field of psychology. Much of the early research took place in the 1970s, and led to an assumption in the field that rewards were ineffective. In 1999, two teams of researchers engaged in a debate over the effects of rewards on motivation. Edward L. Deci and Richard M. Ryan of Rochester University (the cocreators of self-determination theory) strongly recommended against the use of rewards, whereas a team of researchers led by Robert Eisenberger of the University of Delaware argued that the negative effects of rewards are quite limited. Although the two camps of researchers did not see eye to eye, they did find some similar patterns of effects among the complex results of rewards. In many ways, these reward effects demonstrate how external factors—such as praise, criticism, and pressure from parents—can influence children's motivation.

Task-Contingent versus Performance-Contingent Rewards

The Magic Marker study conducted by Mark Lepper and his colleagues at Stanford University utilized a task-contingent reward—meaning the participants are told they'll receive a reward for engaging in the task. On the other hand, a performance-contingent reward is earned by attaining a certain level of achievement. Judy Harackiewicz and her colleagues at the University of Wisconsin–Madison have demonstrated that performance-contingent rewards are more positive (or less negative) than task-contingent rewards. In other words, if you're going to reward children, a trophy for winning first place (performance-contingent) in a tournament is less negative than providing participation trophies to all athletes (task-contingent) as a way to help them feel good. Providing a reward for excellent performance signifies competence, exemplified by an award such as an Olympic gold medal. The medal itself isn't worth nearly as much as what it signifies in terms of world-class performance. Thus, performance-contingent rewards carry with them more meaning, as opposed to the task-contingent rewards my son Jack's friend Hannah, who had six trophies and zero wins, was receiving for playing soccer.

Expected versus Unexpected Rewards

Recall that Mark Lepper's Magic Marker study with five- to six-year-olds compared the effects on intrinsic motivation of an expected task-contingent reward to no reward. Lepper also included a third condition, in which participants received an unexpected reward for drawing with the Magic Markers. Thus, these participants were treated the same way as the no-reward participants at the outset of the experiment, and only after finishing their drawing did they unexpectedly receive a good-player award. This unexpected reward didn't decrease intrinsic motivation, leading the researchers to conclude that because children in the unexpected reward condition didn't think about the reward during the task, their reason for drawing remained intrinsic in nature.

The evidence is quite clear that expected rewards prove more detrimental to motivation because they shift one's thinking during an activity, whereas unexpected rewards do not. One issue with unexpected rewards is whether or not this is a sustainable solution in terms of rewards. In other words, if an athlete receives an unexpected reward, will that shift motivation in the future because the athlete comes to expect rewards for subsequent activity or performances? This is a research question that still needs to be addressed.

Tangible versus Intangible Rewards

Rewards that are tangible (e.g., gold stars, money, or prizes) tend to have more negative effects on intrinsic motivation than intangible rewards (e.g., praise). The more a child thinks about a reward, the more it becomes the focus and takes attention away from the activity. Thus, one way to maintain high levels of intrinsic motivation is to create an environment in which there are few distractions. This helps children focus on the task in which they're engaging.

Boring versus Enjoyable Tasks

In the majority of the cases where rewards are criticized, participants begin with a high level of intrinsic motivation for the activity. This is referred to as a ceiling effect in psychology, because scores on some variable (motivation, in this case) can't go much higher. On the other hand, rewards are unlikely to dampen motivation when participants don't enjoy a task. In those cases, we're dealing with a floor effect—meaning motivation can't get much lower. It makes sense then, that rewards have the potential to benefit motivation in those who don't like an activity by getting them started—but rewards possess the potential to damage to relatively high motivation levels.

Summary of Reward Effects

It's safe to say that there is a consensus among psychologists that expected, tangible, task-contingent rewards for taking part in an enjoyable activity are ill-advised. The young girl my son Jack befriended in Hawaii who had received six trophies without winning a game is likely to focus her attention more on rewards than on improving, working hard, or having fun compared to another child who doesn't receive a reward. If you're going to reward children in athletics, it's better to do so unexpectedly, and in response to good performance. Furthermore, it's wise to utilize intangible rewards such as praise, as opposed to tangible rewards such as trophies.

Of course, praise as a reward carries with it several complications, not the least of which is whether the praise is sincere. The self-esteem movement has led to "good job!" exclamations from parents for tasks as simple as picking up one's clothes or throwing away waste after a meal. The danger with so much praise is that children may begin to expect praise for everything they do, and fail to behave properly in the absence of praise. Not many adults have bosses who praise our every move, and preparing children to expect constant praise is nearly as dangerous as never praising them at all. We owe it to our kids to praise them when they behave well, but also provide them accurate feedback about areas in which they can improve. Once again, it's our job to balance those two basic social needs—the need to feel good and the need to be good (i.e., accurate and appropriate).

In sum, at their worst, rewards are harmful to motivation, and at their best, we should still proceed with caution. If a child shows any interest in an activity, it's better to provide that child autonomy and let that passion grow, rather than provide external incentives such as rewards that may take away attention from the activity at hand. We've seen this anecdotally with Todd Marinovich and his dad and we've seen it empirically with dozens of studies that illustrate the danger of rewards for taking part in an activity one already enjoys. It's worth noting that the majority of the empirical studies on rewards are short sessions of less than an hour. If rewards can have powerfully negative effects after a single administration, imagine the longer-term, cumulative effects rewards may have on children exposed to them on a daily basis. Rewards have the potential to teach children that they ought to work hard only when they have the opportunity to earn a reward, thus diminishing their intrinsic motivation for an activity, and also decreasing their general intrinsic drive to work hard across a variety of situations.

What to Do about Rewards?

Based on the available evidence, we know rewards have the potential to undermine intrinsic motivation. In addition, I caution against anything that shifts the focus of an activity to an extrinsic reward. However, if a child doesn't currently enjoy an activity, a reward can't do too much damage, and in fact may light a motivational spark. As parents, we need to remember that one of the challenges with the use of rewards in sports is that each child is motivated differently, so a blanket motivational approach to all members of a team will probably work for some and not for others. As a coach and professor, one of my greatest challenges is trying to connect with each athlete or student. What works for one may not work for another, and providing individual attention for twenty students or athletes during a class or practice is impossible. Some individuals are intrinsically motivated and don't need a reward whereas others need something external to get them going.

In my first year as the defensive coordinator with the University of St. Thomas men's basketball team, one of our players (let's call him Billy) was less than motivated to work on important aspects of the game, such as staying in an athletic stance, diving for loose balls, boxing out his opponent for a rebound, or doing anything that required exertion on the defensive end of the court. Billy was one of those players who apparently thought that "de-fence" is the thing that goes around a house, not something necessary to win basketball games.

Fresh out of graduate school at the University of Wisconsin, I was pretty sure I had all the answers on how to motivate athletes. Having just finished my dissertation on competition, cooperation, and intrinsic motivation, I was excited to put this research into action. I was (and still am) convinced that finding ways to intrinsically motivate players is critical to a team's success. The problem seemed to be Billy's lack of motivation (either extrinsic or intrinsic) for defense.

After a couple weeks of hollering in futility at Billy to play harder, stopping drills to emphasize the importance of defense as a way to earn trust among teammates and win championships, I felt like a failure, and was worried my job might be in jeopardy if we didn't defend better once games started. I decided an individual meeting with Billy was in order. As Billy sat down in my office, I prepared myself for conflict. After all, we were clearly not on the same page when it came to the motivation and desire to play defense. I hoped we could work things out, but also wanted Billy to know that he wouldn't play if he didn't play defense.

I was shocked by the calm tone in Billy's voice as I explained to him that things didn't have to go the way they were in practice.

"I understand, Coach Tauer," Billy said.

"No, Billy, I don't think you do," I responded. "It doesn't have to be this way. I don't have to yell at you, make you run sprints, do extra push-ups, and point out your lack of hustle in front of the team."

"Really, I understand coach. It's OK. I don't mind," Billy replied.

I continued to explain to Billy that I didn't want to yell at him, and that life for both of us could be simpler and less stressful on the court if Billy would put forth effort on defense. This exchange went back and forth several times, with no progress. I was utterly confused as Billy repeatedly explained that he understood and that he didn't care that I was all over him in practice. Frustrated, and feeling as if Billy and I were speaking different languages, I stopped talking and asked Billy to elaborate as to why he was so accepting of the current state of affairs—which I believed was unhealthy and unpleasant for Billy, me, and the team as we approached our first game.

Billy looked at me and smiled sheepishly. "Coach," Billy said, "I'm lazy. I've always been lazy. I just don't like to play defense. I want us to do well, and I know defense is important, but you're going to have to yell at me if you want me to play hard. It's OK. I know that I need a kick in the butt."

I sat quietly, reflecting at once on (a) the insight Billy had into his own behavior and motivation, (b) my lingering confusion why Billy wouldn't simply work harder, and (c) my sudden realization that coaching was going to be a bit more complicated than I had thought. We ended up going 24–4 that season, won the conference championship, qualified for the NCAA Division III National Tournament, and exceeded most people's expectations. Billy had a solid season, the best of his career, and he was also right on in his evaluation of himself. He needed a kick in the butt semiregularly, and seemed to play harder (and better) when this happened.

As teachers, coaches, and parents, we hope that those we mentor will be intrinsically motivated. This is not always the case. One of our great challenges is to figure out what makes different individuals tick, and then to find ways to create an environment that facilitates high levels of motivation in students, athletes, employees, and children. Motivation requires a fit between an individual and that individual's environment. A one-size-fits-all approach simply will not work.

Motivating the Already Motivated Athlete

What if you're the parent of a child whose coach uses rewards and punishments to motivate and your child is already intrinsically motivated? How can you protect your child from the overjustification effect? In one compelling demonstration, Russ Fazio conducted a study very similar to Mark Lepper's Magic Marker study. He added one wrinkle to it, though, by placing a previously taken picture of the child drawing in front of him or her. Before they began drawing, Fazio asked individuals in this group to describe the photo that showed them drawing with markers, and asked them to explain why they were drawing with the markers when the picture was taken. The purpose of this was to make salient in their minds the idea that they enjoyed drawing with markers. This simple step kept their intrinsic motivation high, even when they were subsequently rewarded in the experiment. It demonstrated a cheap and easy way to remind people that doing what they love is both good and admirable.

As parents we won't be able to eliminate all forms of rewards in our children's lives. However, we can work to keep them focused and attentive on why they enjoy the activities they do. This will reduce the likelihood that their intrinsic motivation will be damaged by rewards, praise, parental pressure, or other external factors.

Recently, I received an email from a longtime camper's father. The camper, let's call him Chris, is an absolute gym rat. As a junior in high school, he tried out for the varsity and made the team, but was playing very little. He was frustrated because many of the other players ahead of him hadn't worked nearly as hard, and several of them had serious disciplinary issues at school. His father, Will, was concerned because he saw Chris's passion for basketball dying a quick death. He asked me how to deal with this, and my response focused on two things I thought Will could do to help Chris. First, I encouraged Will to keep Chris talking about his love of the game. If Will could get Chris to focus on what he loved about basketball, I thought that would make the negative aspects of his current situation seem less daunting. This can be tough, especially if the practice environment is less than motivating. (I had no way of knowing if this was the case, but it seemed probable given the circumstances.) Chris needed to find a way to continue to practice with passion every day, because that was his only chance to show the coaches that he deserved more playing time. I also encouraged Will to remind Chris that one of the major purposes of sports is to learn from difficult and challenging situations. I've seen lots of players get burned out in similar situations, while many others continue to pursue their dreams. I suggested that Will talk to Chris about ways he can better himself as a player and person through this whole experience. I felt it was important to get Chris focused on those larger goals right away, because it's usually too late once a player gets fed up with the whole experience.

Two days later, I received an email back from Chris's dad. He wrote me, "Your email had a super positive effect on Chris—I had a great conversation with him on Wednesday night and he came home from Thursday's practice focused in a good mood." Chris ended up breaking his school's record for three-point baskets made in a game the next season, and he went on to play college basketball.

Motivating athletes is at once an art and a science. We can't forget that each child, each athlete, is unique—and spending time talking with them, hearing them out, encouraging them, and challenging them are all ways we can nurture their development in sports and in life. The judicious use of external motivators is critical, lest we see our children wind up like Latrell Sprewell, unwilling to play a game they used to love because millions aren't enough. Whether we're talking about parents or coaches placing pressure on a child or external rewards such as trophies or money stealing focus from an activity, there are many ways to squelch a child's interest by allowing good intentions to turn into overinvolvement that children perceive as unpleasant pressure. Our job as parents is to encourage and facilitate our children as they chase their passions—and then be careful to step back and allow them to savor these passions.

Words of Wisdom for WOSPs

1. Encourage your children to chase their passions. It may be helpful to ask your children periodically why they're passionate about the activities they love. This can help refocus their energy on the healthy motivations for pursuing an activity, and steer them clear of an extrinsic focus.

2. Ask yourself if your children are already motivated. If so, there should be no need for external motivators. If not, some external motivator may be a useful way to build excitement for an activity, at least in the short term. Ask yourself if you've ever rewarded your children for simply doing something they already enjoy.

3. If you use rewards, be careful. They have the potential to undermine intrinsic motivation. In addition, parental overinvolvement can function similarly to rewards or punishment because it can add external pressure.

7

"Sports Are Life, The Rest Is Just Details":
What Happened to the Real Goals of Youth Sports?

Several years back, an athletic company started a line of T-shirts that bore the phrase, "Basketball is life, the rest is just details." Before long, the shirts were available for virtually any sport a child might play. Whether it was soccer, football, softball, or even cheerleading, these shirts promoted the idea that it is entirely acceptable for sports to be the focus of one's life. In fact, someone from another culture who took the shirts literally might be confused, wondering which shirt was accurate. Do soccer, basketball, softball, football, volleyball, or cheerleading truly define life? Interestingly, there were no "Math is life" shirts, or "Reading is life" shirts, nor were there shirts bearing the slogans, "Family is life," "Being a good sport is life," "Developing character is life," or "Being a good person is life." Apparently, these goals weren't deemed marketable enough for children. What message do slogans such as these send children about the relative importance of athletics? If the true goal of sports is to develop values and skills that will serve one well for a lifetime, it's shortsighted to approach a sport as an end in itself.

Although this line of "Sports are life" T-shirts appear to take things to an extreme, many children's lives seem to follow that mantra. Whether it is the child playing seventy-five baseball games per summer, the volleyball player who suffers chronic tendonitis because she plays the sport year-round, or the swimmer who is in the pool every morning at 5:00 a.m., countless childhoods are focused on the pursuit of athletic excellence and/or monetary reward. Each year at basketball camp I ask the campers how many of them would like to grow up to be professional basketball players. (I don't ask them if $21 million will be enough to feed their family.) Virtually every boy in camp responds "Yes." Furthermore, many of them think they'll accomplish this goal, even though the probability of them making the NBA is incredibly low. Girls are noticeably less likely to say "yes" to having a desire to play professional sports. I am not certain why this is the case, but my hunch is that it has something to do with the amount of money, attention, and prestige NBA players receive compared to WNBA players. It's also possible girls simply have more balanced views of the world, and sports define life for boys more than girls. Why is it that so many children, particularly boys, would rather be pro athletes than successful businesspeople, lawyers, teachers, doctors, or engineers? Is it fame, fortune, or fun?

This emphasis on athletics is not entirely new, but the ferocity with which parents and children have chased their dreams through sports has evolved over the past several decades. As we discussed, athletes such as Todd Marinovich, Andre Agassi, and Tiger Woods, and their respective fathers, helped shift the cultural pendulum to reward and recognize the training of athletic prodigies. At least three factors have conspired to trigger this sequence of events: success, attention, and money.

Early Success for Young Athletes

Recently, a growing number of athletes have experienced extraordinary success in their sports at a young age. Tiger Woods won more tournaments at a younger age than anyone in history. The Williams sisters had unprecedented success in tennis before they were out of their teens. LeBron James was named to the NBA All-Star team and led the Cleveland Cavaliers to the NBA Finals in what should have been his senior year of college. These are just some of the examples of prodigious young athletes excelling beyond their years.

In decades past, sports such as women's figure skating and gymnastics saw young athletes ascend to prominence, in large part due to the physical advantages of youth in certain sports. Quite simply, it's easier for a sixteen-year-old female than a twenty-five-year-old to perform many of the movements required in these sports. However, in sports requiring speed and strength, youth has typically been an impediment until an athlete reaches his or her physical peak. In most sports, that physical peak is somewhere in the mid- to late twenties. Today, we're seeing younger and younger athletes in all major sports, more prepared physically and mentally than athletes generations before them. However, there are also more demands on athletes than ever before when it comes to media pressure, publicity, and people clamoring for their attention. As such, even though young athletes may be more prepared than before, they're still unlikely to be prepared for the media maelstrom they will encounter when they make their professional debuts.

Media Attention

A remarkable amount of media attention has been given to child sports prodigies. Case studies of extreme behavior make good news in today's society. The Williams sisters grew up in Compton, California, one of the nation's notoriously rough cities. They beat the odds in large part due to endless sessions on the tennis courts with their father. While the media may attempt to use these stories as inspirations, we need to question whether this is the example that we want to inspire countless other parents to believe they can do the same thing. Well-intentioned parents internalize powerful lessons from Earl Woods, Marv Marinovich, Mike Agassi, and Richard Williams: Start our children younger, work our children harder and longer, train our children better, and they will be the next great young stars. The two major problems lie in whether or not a young child endorses this goal, and what portion of their life are they willing to spend pursuing the long odds that often accompany the goal of sports superstardom?

Wealth

In addition to their on-court achievements, these prodigious young athletes all are wealthy beyond belief. It's estimated Tiger Woods has made over $1 billion in his career so far; the Williams sisters are reported to be worth a combined $200 million; Andre Agassi was making more than $25 million per year in endorsements at the height of his career; and LeBron James signed a $90 million contract to endorse Nike shoes before he graduated from high school! Between hopes of prestige, success, and financial security, it's no wonder parents eagerly plot ways to develop their children into the next great superstars. Of course, the odds of a young athlete making the professional ranks in a given sport are incredibly slim.

The National Collegiate Athletic Association (NCAA) reports that approximately 2 percent of high school athletes receive college athletic scholarships.[21] Unbeknownst to most, many of those scholarships only partially cover tuition. In 2008, the average athletic scholarship was $10,409 per year.[22] Thus, the average return for a high school athlete is approximately $500 per year. That hardly covers the equipment, much less the travel, team fees, camp fees, personal trainers, and gym memberships. Sadly, I've had parents of student athletes tell me they cannot afford college and need an athletic scholarship for their son because they invested so much money in his athletic career.

Furthermore, the minute odds of playing professional athletics are even more staggering. In men's basketball, three in 10,000 high

---

21. "Behind the Blue Disk," 2012, http://www.ncaa.org/sites/default/files/ NCAA%2BAthletics%2BScholarships.pdf.

22. Bill Pennington, "Expectations Lose to Reality of Sports Scholarships," *New York Times*, March 10, 2008, http://www.nytimes.com/2008/03/10/ sports/10scholarships.html?pagewanted=all.

school players make the NBA; in women's basketball, two in 10,000 high school players make the WNBA; in football, eight in 10,000 high school players make the NFL; in baseball, fifty in 10,000 get drafted, yet only ten of 10,000 ever make the major leagues. Quite simply, the financial return on the investment of youth sports is abysmal. Given the proven poor return, why are so many parents and their children delusional when it comes to the likelihood and value of college athletic scholarships?

The Overconfidence Bias

Due to our drive to feel good, we tend to be optimistic, often overly so. This can be seen in virtually every aspect of life in which we tend to think we're better than we actually are. In class, I do a demonstration where I ask students to rate themselves, compared to their classmates, on a scale of zero to one hundred in two areas, friendliness and work ethic. Because I have them rate themselves compared to their classmates, we should have half the students above fifty and half below fifty. Assuming friendliness and work ethic are not correlated, only 25 percent of students should be above average on both measures. Instead, typically 95 percent of students say they're above average in both friendliness and work ethic. Statistically, this is virtually impossible, yet that's how they rate themselves semester after semester.

Examples of overconfidence can be seen throughout society, in business professionals, teachers, students, and pro athletes. Why does this overconfidence bias exist? Our desire to feel good leads us to seek out information that places us in the best possible light. As a result, parents of young athletes are likely to pay attention to their children's good plays, and compare their children to less capable players. This selective attention on the part of parents leads them to have inflated views of their children's abilities. Thus it's no surprise when parents and children are so often upset that they're not playing enough, getting enough shots, getting to pitch enough innings, or getting to throw enough passes.

The Availability Heuristic

As humans, our basic need to be right leads us to consider many factors in making decisions. However, because our world moves so quickly, we typically have limited time to make decisions. So we often make snap decisions based on how quickly information comes to our minds. In some cases, this process is efficient and accurate; in others, it can lead us astray. Social psychologists refer to this tendency to overestimate the frequency of an event due to the ease with which an example comes to mind as the availability heuristic.

As described earlier in the book, the availability heuristic helps us understand why people fear airplane crashes more than car crashes, even though far more people die in car accidents each year. (The media contributes mightily to the availability heuristic.) This heuristic also helps explain why we fear other accidents more than cancer or heart disease, even though these are the two most common causes of death in our country. When it comes to youth sports, parents who want the best for their children find it easy to recall times their children played well. This biased processing leads parents to behave irrationally, and to overestimate the ability and likelihood of success their child will have in youth sports.

The Confirmation Bias

Despite the staggeringly thin odds, most parents and children drastically inflate the chances of making it to the professional ranks, even in the face of objective information that demonstrates those odds are close to zero. How do parents maintain the view that their child is outstanding? When motivated to see their children in a positive light, parents actively search for information consistent with this belief. Once we believe something to be true—especially when we believe it in the face of contradictory evidence—it's virtually impossible for us to be convinced otherwise. Take the person you meet and they come across as hostile and angry. It will likely take many additional interactions before you perceive him or her differently, and rarely will we give that person many chances to undo our existing impression.

Pass the Rose-Colored Lenses

The overconfidence bias, availability heuristic, and confirmation bias all connect to the mental spin parents can put on their children's abilities. These cognitive tricks combine to provide each of us with a unique and subjective perception of reality. When sports fans of opposing teams watch a game, they frequently argue over which team got cheated by the refs and which team committed more penalties or fouls. These perceptions of reality are rarely random. Rather, they tend to be motivated by our desire to feel good.

Several years ago, a coach forwarded me an email from a parent. The parent wrote several paragraphs of descriptors about his son, and why he deserved to be on the "A" Traveling Basketball Team. The dad went through the family lineage, highlighting athletic accomplishments for the boy's five siblings as well as his parents. The dad described the boy in terms generally reserved for world-class athletes (e.g., runs like a gazelle, shoots like a rifleman). The dad went on and on and on describing his son's statistics, physical features, vertical jump, and even his baseball and soccer stats from the past season. The dad even went so far as to include his own stats from high school basketball twenty-five years earlier. He concluded his message with: "His basketball gifts are significantly more apparent than those of his older sister, who would probably still be with the program if she could have made an A team. That's water under the bridge, but I can't have that happen to my son. At a minimum, I will need his college basketball scholarship money."

The most frightening detail? The boy was in third grade at the time! How terrifying that, despite clear evidence that expecting a high return on investment is foolhardy, parents count on young athletes providing money in the way of athletic scholarships before the kids are ten years old. We all want the best for our children, but to help them we must first take off the rose-colored lenses and realize who our kids are and what we want for them in a big-picture sense. The conclusion to the story? The boy never played one minute of varsity basketball. Imagine how much time and energy was spent by this dad, and how much pressure was placed on this young athlete to excel at a level that was probably unattainable for him from the outset.

So if parents are able to delude themselves in the face of terrible odds, we begin to understand why so many parents spend such inordinate amounts of time encouraging children to participate in sports. In Chapters 3 and 4, we discussed two basic social needs: to feel good and to be good. The desire for young athletes to attain success, prestige, and even financial wealth would all fall into the category of being good. Furthermore, implicit in many parents' thinking about sports is, "If my children are successful, they'll be happy." In other words, "If my children play a lot and play well, they'll also feel good about themselves." Thus, we observe two goals that lead parents to encourage too many organized, competitive sports: a desire to see their children feel good about themselves and a desire to see their children excel. In some cases, these goals stem from parents' frustrations about shortcomings in their own athletic careers. In most cases, however, parents mean well and want the best for their children, but go to unfortunate extremes in the pursuit of childhood athletic excellence.

As a college basketball coach, I spend quite a bit of time recruiting high school students to attend the University of St. Thomas. This includes attending their games; phone, text, and email contacts with players and coaches; and visits to campus by players and parents. Over the years, I've developed close friendships with many high school basketball coaches. Most high school coaches teach as a full-time job, and receive a relatively small stipend for coaching. If one calculates the wage high school coaches are paid per hour, it's typically right around the minimum wage. Many of these coaches go to extreme lengths to do right by their players. Beyond the countless hours in practices and games, summer open gyms, and film work, this may also mean providing extra rides and meals, lending a supportive ear, or helping student athletes navigate the college selection process. In the wake of all this time and effort expended by coaches, one would expect that they'd be showered with gratitude. Instead, I'm continually surprised by the frequency with which they're confronted by hostile parents.

Recently, I was at a game recruiting when I bumped into a former high school rival of mine whom I hadn't seen in fifteen years. He's now coaching a varsity girls' team at a local high school. I asked him how his game had gone earlier that evening. "Not so well," he responded glumly.

I asked if they had lost, and he nodded, and continued, "But that's not what's bugging me. After the game I was screamed at by a parent for several minutes." He appeared quite shaken by the incident, so in the service of this book, I questioned him about the events leading to this confrontation.

"Her mom is mad because the girl isn't playing enough," he said.

When I asked if the girl was one of his better players, he shrugged and said, "Quite honestly, she's our fifteenth player on a fifteen-player roster. She's a great kid. I should have kept a more talented junior, but I chose to keep this girl because she's a senior, she has a great attitude, and she's worked really hard for three years. I guess that backfired."

I wished him well, but couldn't get over how much this was bothering him. He makes ends meet on a teacher's salary, invests incredible energy into coaching, and then receives the reward of being berated after a tough loss by a parent whose child made the team primarily because she has a good attitude. With a mom like that, it's a minor miracle the player turned out with as great an attitude as she did. It's unfortunate that nobody ever told the mother that her daughter is an average player with a phenomenal attitude, and that she should be proud of what a wonderful person and teammate her daughter is.

Sadly, I've heard dozens of stories just like this one. Why is it that parents will accost coaches, yet rarely do I hear a parent complain about a teacher? Sure, there are cases where parents believe a teacher has it out for a child, in the same way some parents believe a coach just doesn't like their son or daughter. However, a major difference in the coaching and teaching professions is that at the end of each day, a coach sees a *win* or a *loss* as an objective marker of success or failure. In addition, fans everywhere (depending on the team's popularity) see the same thing. Imagine if teachers walked out of a classroom each day and everyone in the school, and in the local community, knew if that teacher had a good day or bad day, and whether they had outperformed another teacher from their rival school.

Let's take this a step further and imagine that teachers competed against other teachers and their classrooms each day. Some days the teachers won, other days they lost. Then imagine that people expected every day to be a good one, took this for granted, and piled criticism on the teacher whenever the classroom day was deemed a loss. Would that be a good thing? Parents have raised expectations of their children's coaches to unattainable levels, shifting the focus from their children's development to perfection defined in terms of wins and losses.

In 2009, the St. Thomas men's basketball team won our first thirty games. We were ranked number one in the nation in Division III, before losing to the eventual national champion, Washington University, in the national quarterfinals. Washington University had won the national title the year before, so losing a tough game to them was no embarrassment. When we returned from the tournament, the question we were asked repeatedly was simple: "What happened?" It was as if people were in disbelief that we'd lost a game, even to the two-time national champions.

While dichotomizing the world into wins and losses is dangerous, the reality is that these are the primary criteria through which most coaches are evaluated. I've never met a coach who intentionally plays players who reduce the likelihood of winning. In fact, as best as they can, coaches play the players who provide the best opportunity for a team to be successful. There may be subpar coaches out there; however, most are very competitive people who despise losing. Thus, it would be surprising to see any high school or college coach who would play someone the coach didn't think gave the team the best chance to win.

One of the difficulties of judging everything in terms of wins and losses is that by definition, competition is a zero-sum situation in which one individual or team must win and one must lose. As a result, parents, spectators, fans, players, and coaches are all naïve to think they can win all of the time. In addition, the bar to measure success is always rising. Once a team moves from the bottom of the standings to average, fans expect that team to remain at or above this level. Essentially, fans expect their team to perform as well or better than they ever have before each and every season, jumping on a hedonic treadmill of sorts. This phenomenon is not limited to sports, but the media attention sports receive certainly makes teams and individual athletes prime candidates for these unrealistic expectations.

Several years ago, I visited the University of Wisconsin–Madison's basketball coaches. The Badgers have traditionally been downtrodden in basketball, advancing to the NCAA tournament only twice in the fifty-year span from 1946 to 1996. Dick Bennett led them to the NCAA tourney three times between 1997 and 2000, including a Final Four appearance in 2000. Even though the Badgers had more success in that four-year period than the previous fifty years, Badger fans were unhappy with the slow pace of Bennett's team. Even when coaches win, they lose. Before the NCAA tournament in 2000, many fans were fed up with Bennett and the Badger's slow pace of play. Of course, winning the regional and advancing to the Final Four fixed that in a hurry.

Bo Ryan took over the Wisconsin program in 2001. Over the past decade plus, Coach Ryan has taken the University of Wisconsin to unparalleled levels of success. Ryan's teams won four Division III NCAA championships at the University of Wisconsin–Platteville. In fact, in my sophomore year as an undergraduate, my team at the University of St. Thomas lost in the Sweet Sixteen to Ryan's UW–Platteville team. Simply put, Ryan's was the model Division III program in the country. He moved to coach UW–Milwaukee (a Division I school), and after three strong years there, he was hired for his dream job at the University of Wisconsin–Madison. Wisconsinites are noted for being some of the more avid fans in the country, and having a basketball team they can be proud of has been a real feather in their cap. In 2007, the Badgers ascended to the number-one ranking in the country for a short time, before losing to Big Ten rival Ohio State, which was ranked in the top three in the nation. The next week, the Badgers lost a road game to Michigan State, another top-notch team. The response? Irate fans called the basketball office and left obscene voicemails that questioned how in the world the Badgers could ever lose to a team like Michigan State? (Keep in mind Michigan State was the same team that had dominated the Big Ten for the past decade and went on to win the national championship.) This is just another in a long list of examples of how quickly the bar for success can get raised, with fans expecting perfection. Bo Ryan is generally considered one of the top basketball coaches in the entire country and his losses still attract immense criticism in this what-have-you-done-for-me-lately world.

Of course, this phenomenon of unrealistic expectations is not entirely new. John Wooden, the legendary coach at UCLA from 1948 to 1975, won ten NCAA championships during a twelve-year span at the end of his coaching career. It's unlikely this record will ever be matched. In Wooden's penultimate season as a coach, 1973–74, his team lost in the national tournament. After having won nine of the previous ten national championships, Wooden was perceived by some to have lost it as a coach. (Keep in mind that only two teams have earned the men's Division I national championship in consecutive years in the forty years since Wooden's team repeated that accomplishment for seven consecutive years.) Wooden's team came back the following season and won the 1975 national championship. After the game, one of the first responses he received was from an alumnus who offered the following congratulations: "Congratulations, Coach. You let us down last year, but this made up for it."[23]

Imagine the pressure when ten titles in twelve years still isn't good enough. There are more than three hundred Division I programs and only one wins the championship. With five coaches and fifteen players on each team, nationwide there are 1,500 coaches and 4,500 players investing incredible amounts of time and effort. Are all but one considered a failure? With this mentality, what defines success? If winning the championship game is the only measure of success, then the system is such that 99.7 percent are going to fail, leading to unending criticism.

Parents also send strong messages to children about what's truly important through their interactions with their children. If parents attend every game and many practices, and the parent hires a personal trainer to further hone the child's skills, and on car rides home the parent asks question after question about the game, yet doesn't regularly ask about the courses a child is taking or get involved in the child's academic world, it doesn't take long for that child to realize how to receive attention. The parent who analyzes every play of the game on the ride home may be the same parent gabbing on his cell phone after picking his daughter up from school.

Children's age-old response to "What did you do today at school?" is often "Not much." It's possible that this response is accurate—that little goes on in school. However, my hunch is that many children provide that answer because at some point they picked up on cues that their parents don't really want to know a lot of information about what the child is studying in school relative to their desire to know more

---

23. Seth Davis, *Wooden: A Coach's Life*, (New York: Times Books, 2014), 440.

about the child's sports. Consider the following hypothetical conversation between a parent and a child:

PARENT. Did you talk about the presidential election today?

CHILD. Yes.

PARENT. Which candidate did most of your classmates side with?

CHILD. I don't know.

A different line of questioning that demonstrates a genuine interest on the part of a parent would be much more likely to elicit a thoughtful response. Take the following conversation in which a parent asks questions that indicate the parent is aware of what a class is discussing, and asks questions that require more than one or two word responses.

PARENT. What do you think of the US's decision to invade Iraq?

CHILD. I don't think they should be there.

PARENT. Why not?

CHILD. Because lots of things make it hard for us to solve other countries' problems. Maybe they don't want our help.

PARENT. So what would you do if you were in charge?

CHILD. I don't know. What do you think?

Now the tables are turned and the parent is in the difficult position of having to provide a thoughtful answer, where "not much" will simply not do. Recently, my son Jack began probing about cells and the human body. After my brief—and certainly incomplete—explanation, Jack continued with more questions about molecules and atoms, and what atoms are made of. If parents want to engage their children, we need to ask questions that require answers to the "why" questions that promote critical thinking and communication skills in our children. We also need to be willing to not have all the answers, and be open to seeking them out in collaboration with our children. Jack and I ended up searching the Internet for more information, and I think he and I both learned a valuable lesson. Instead of a focus on developing our children's thinking skills, too many parent-child conversations focus on the scoreboard at an athletics event.

So how can parents encourage athletic participation but also teach valuable lessons? As one mother of a camper recently wrote to me, "In terms of raising children right, if we raise them to be athletes, they'll be ill-prepared for much of life. However, if we raise them to be parents, spouses, friends, and hard workers, then they'll be prepared to succeed throughout all phases of their lives." Not surprisingly, the woman's daughter has a vigor, curiosity, positive attitude, and drive to experience life that stands out immediately. The mother's proposed approach makes a lot of sense, and it highlights how far we have gotten from the goals of sports. Many of the intended goals of youth sports fall into the categories listed by the mother, yet it is painfully obvious that on a daily basis, the emphasis is clearly on sports, competition, and winning, as opposed to the lessons that can be learned from sports.

One need not look far to be convinced that sports are emphasized in our culture. Pick up any morning newspaper across the country and you'll see an entire section of the paper dedicated to sports. Watch any news broadcast and you'll see an entire segment devoted to sports. In many cases, there are specific pages or segments devoted solely to high school athletics. On the other hand, academics typically receive one day per year in our local paper when the top students at local high schools are listed. Each year, *Parade* magazine highlights approximately forty volleyball, basketball, baseball, and softball players around the country for their excellence in sports. This year, they also had an issue devoted to All-Americans in Service. These were students around the nation who worked to enact change in their communities. The stories were inspiring and amazing. The feature also got me thinking about how many children would be more motivated to participate and lead service projects if they realized service was as valued as hitting a ball or making a basket.

What message are children learning when at seven years old, they realize the majority of attention is heaped on star high school athletes, not star high school students. Of course, attention should not be the incentive that drives behavior, yet we know children are very attuned to behaviors that bring pleasing outcomes to them. Google "athletics" and one will find nearly 160 million hits. Google "academics" and find less than half that amount. While not scientific, this illustrates the ingrained emphasis on sports in our culture. Of course, as we discussed in Chapter 2, there are many benefits that can be derived from sports, and if these are achieved, maybe this societal preoccupation with sports will serve young athletes well.

Competition

The value our culture places on competition is evident with even a cursory examination of the media coverage of sports. In a capitalistic culture, competition is often lauded as a backbone of society. What are the outcomes of an inordinate emphasis on competition? The benefits include an appreciation of challenge, goal setting, and resilience. On the other hand, this can also breed a mindset that focuses only on winning, at the expense of improvement and skill development. This can lead to a culture of children who worry more if they won or lost than why they won or lost, and figuring out how to improve in the future.

Take, for example, a friend whose nephew played on a baseball team in New York. This ten-year-old group of players met sixty-one times during the summer. They played sixty games and had one practice! How many times did they work on skills development, such as fielding ground balls, laying down bunts, or practicing first-and-third situations? My hunch is rarely, if ever. Instead, the players would learn to focus on areas they're good at and avoid those that they aren't.

The scene may be worse in basketball. Until the past fifteen years, youth basketball typically consisted of grade schools playing twenty to thirty games against other local grade schools. Today, the youth basketball landscape is markedly different due to the proliferation of traveling and AAU basketball. The benefits of these programs include more opportunities for competition and increased exposure to college scouts. Of course, AAU basketball hasn't led to the opening of additional universities, so the number of available scholarships hasn't changed. Instead, the additional exposure likely benefits players from smaller towns and states who wouldn't otherwise be on a college recruiter's recruiting map, while likely hurting players from larger metropolitan areas whose proximity already makes it relatively easy to recruit in those areas. There aren't more scholarships, but there's a lot more money being invested to compete for those scholarship dollars.

On the face of it, having more opportunities seems like a good thing. But what do those opportunities come at the expense of in terms of time, money, and other potential opportunities? A few years ago, I was conducting a girls' basketball camp for high school players. One of the players, Katie, consistently missed camp on Monday evenings. When Tuesday came around, I asked her where she had been. She replied, "We have traveled to tournaments the past three weeks.

We leave Thursday, arrive Friday, play eight games over the weekend, and return Sunday evening. I was just too exhausted. Plus, I had to lift weights Monday morning, and go to soccer Monday afternoon." While more effort tends to be better, there is a law of diminishing returns. In most cases, AAU teams involve far more games than practices. This is just another example of competition trumping skill development. It makes perfect sense that Katie would yearn for a day off from basketball. At what point does a young athlete acknowledge that more isn't better? If our children are spending all their time traveling and playing games, to the point that they have little energy for anything else, when do they expect to actually focus on skill development? So much effort is expended demonstrating competence in games and tournaments that developing competence seems to have fallen by the wayside.

Fixed versus Growth Mindsets: The Dark Side of Competition

This nearly exclusive focus on competition leads to two problems. First, skill development has taken a backseat, to the point where our young athletes who show great promise in grade school often plateau during middle school and high school. This shouldn't be surprising since excellence at anything from basketball to playing the piano requires thousands and thousands of repetitions. If a talented six-foot ten-year-old decides he doesn't need to develop his skills dribbling with his left hand because he's too powerful and big to be stopped by his peers, what happens if he doesn't grow? He becomes a six-foot seventeen-year-old who's not very big or powerful, and still can't dribble with his left hand.

I'm not surprised by the influx of foreign-born players in the NBA. While American athletes have focused on dunking, jumping, and playing one on one, players in Europe have focused on skill development. As one colleague of mine in college basketball put it, "Most Europeans spend an hour a day working on one move, over and over and over. Most American players have never spent one consecutive hour of their life perfecting the same move." In our ultrafast society, attention to skills development has decreased in the same way that our attention spans have. There's no substitute for repetitions performed under game-like situations. Unfortunately, our culture's focus on competition has led our young athletes to stray from true skills-development opportunities. The problem with playing only games is that in many games, actual opportunities for growth and development are limited.

A second, wider-ranging problem with this focus on competition is that children grow up with little appreciation for the price that must be paid for excellence. Venus Williams is a gifted athlete, but her vicious serve was honed through more than a million serves. Michael Jordan was nearly unstoppable on the basketball court, yet it took him millions of shots to get there. In the same way that concert pianists are a rare combination of natural gifts and unparalleled work ethic, so too are those who attain supreme excellence in sport.

Unfortunately, in our culture of immediate gratification, children want to be good—they want to be great—and they don't want to wait. They want success now. If hitting a baseball is difficult, why not just play with the Nintendo Wii? With television, the Internet, video games, and text messaging, there are so many distractions for children that it is understandable why an hour of left-handed lay-ups would seem like an eternity. The problem is that a basic-skill deficiency goes away only with (a) a belief in the importance of the skill, and (b) thousands of repetitions.

In basketball, the ability to use both hands equally well is a tremendous advantage. If one can shoot, drive right, and drive left, defenders are at the mercy of the offensive player. As a result, I frequently remind our players of the importance of being able to shoot and dribble with both hands. However, when it comes down to a game, players typically revert to their well-rehearsed movements, meaning most players will shoot lay-ups with their stronger hand, even though it makes it much easier for a defender to block the shot. In the absence of focused practice and repetitions, a player is unlikely to ever try the skill in a game.

Near the end of one season, we were spending five minutes per day on left-handed lay-ups to emphasize the advantage it provides. We were in the midst of a tie game in the conference playoff championship when our back-up center, Alex McCoy, got the ball. Alex is a six-foot-three, two-hundred-sixty-five-pound post player. He's unique in that position because of his relatively short stature. Alex was noted for a move that combined a shot fake, pivot, and right-handed lay-up (known in basketball as an "up and under" move). This was our third game against this opponent, and they were well aware of Alex's go-to move. They practiced against it, and every time he touched the ball their coaches were yelling, "Don't go for the fake! Watch the up-and-under!" To their (and my) surprise, he didn't fake this time, but attempted a left-handed lay-up that he made easily. He looked at me as he ran back down the court with a huge grin. He made several baskets in a row, and finished the game with seventeen points in only nineteen minutes off the bench. Alex was named the Conference Player of the Week and the win catapulted us to the national tournament. To this day, I believe much of Alex's success that day came from the confidence he derived from making a left-handed basket. The next day in practice, I complimented him on his outstanding play, and he said, "Once I made that lay-up, I felt like I couldn't be stopped!"

Of course, if Alex had been afraid to try the lay-up, he never would have made it. His mindset needed to change. In 2006, Carol S. Dweck, a social psychologist at Stanford University, published a book titled simply, *Mindset*. In this exquisitely written volume, Dweck makes the distinction between fixed and growth mindsets. A fixed mindset is one that leads people to believe that abilities are fixed and determined. "I'm not good at math," "I can't shoot left-handed lay-ups," and "I'm not popular" are statements characteristic of a fixed mindset. On the other hand, a growth mindset leads people to believe that they can improve in all areas, and that innate ability is only part of the equation. Those with a growth mindset would be more likely to say, "I need to work harder in math," or "After I practice left-handed lay-ups, I'll be ready to use my left hand in games," or "I'm going to work on meeting more people." Dweck documents incredible stories of improvement among those with a growth mindset. Interestingly, those with a fixed mindset tend to do quite well—until they face a difficult situation. Then, in the face of failure, the fixed mindset that has always reminded a child he or she is good, now conveys the opposite information.

Throughout this chapter, I've highlighted how too much focus on competition and/or winning can be dangerous, even unhealthy. When researchers have examined the effects of competition on intrinsic motivation, many have found evidence to suggest that an external focus on winning will decrease intrinsic motivation. In Alfie Kohn's 1986 book, *No Contest: The Case against Competition*, he highlights the dark side of competition. However, some research indicates that the type of competition, and who is doing the competing also play major roles in the experience of competition. For example, in one study, researchers told one group of competitors to "try to win" and another group to "focus all their energy on winning."[24] The external focus on winning led the second group to demonstrate lower levels of intrinsic motivation. In sum, an intense focus on winning, as opposed to the task at hand, can undermine both intrinsic motivation and performance.

Achievement Motivation and Competition

Achievement motivation is marked by the desire to seek out challenges, surpass standards of excellence, and outperform others. In our research, we have found that individuals high in achievement motivation (HAMs) respond more favorably to competition than individuals low in achievement motivation (LAMs). HAMs appear more excited and challenged by competition than LAMs. As a result, when it comes to youth sports, different individuals may respond differently to competition.

In addition, many studies of competition isolate the effects in the absence of cooperation. The situations in those studies differ from the majority of the competitive activities in which youths participate, which require cooperation with teammates in competition against another team. I've studied this type of competition (intergroup competition) in my summer basketball camp for several years. We found clear and consistent results that participants in the intergroup competition that combined cooperation and competition enjoyed the activity

---

24. Johnmarshall Reeve and Edward L. Deci, "Elements of the competitive situation that affect intrinsic motivation," *Personality and Social Psychology Bulletin 22*, no. 1 (January 1996): 24–33.

more than participants in either a purely competitive or cooperative condition. Thus, while competition has the potential to undermine intrinsic motivation—for those high in achievement motivation, or those competing as part of a team, it appears there may not be only a dark side to competition.

In fact, there are countless examples of lessons learned through competition. These parallel many of the lessons we want our children to learn through youth sports. Whether it be teamwork, persistence, unselfishness, discipline, or winning and losing with grace, competition has the ability to push people to greater heights than they would have dreamed. As Carol Dweck articulates so persuasively in *Mindset*, so much of our responses to painful lessons are framed by our mindsets. If a child responds to losing by sobbing or fighting, it's unlikely he gained anything from the experience. On the other hand, if he realizes he has room for improvement and figures out how to work on things, the sky may be the limit for his potential to grow and improve.

Vince Flynn and Mindsets

Novelist Vince Flynn (1966–2013) graduated from the University of St. Thomas as a well-known football player at the school. Unsure of what to do with his career, he took a job in corporate America with Kraft Foods. Dissatisfied with the position, he bounced around at a couple more jobs, but continued feeling disillusioned. He quit his day job, took up bartending, and spent his days writing a book, a seemingly odd choice given that he had dyslexia and had always found reading and writing difficult.

Fourteen books later, Flynn was a regular on the *New York Times* best-seller list, noted for his thrillers centered on terrorism and read by intelligence specialists around the world. To what did Flynn attribute his success? "I never realized through all of this how competitive I am. I just thought this is how everyone grew up with four brothers and two athletic sisters, all pounding the heck out of each other, never liking to lose. And that is what really saw me through the hardest part of this," said Flynn.[25] He came to his dyslexia as a gift of creativity and insight, which may be one reason he knows how TV dramas will conclude just a few minutes into a show. Flynn's books frequently focus on radical Islamic fundamentalists, and they even had a chillingly prophetic take on terrorism four years before the 9/11 terrorist attacks. In fact, according to Flynn's website, vinceflynn.com, one CIA official told his employees, "I want you to read Flynn's books and start thinking about how we can more effectively wage this war on terror."

Vince Flynn took the lessons he learned from competition and put them to good use in overcoming a learning disability and in his life. It's our job to help our children do the same—embrace competition as a vehicle to improve ourselves, challenge each other, and learn to be better people. If we do this, then sports isn't life, winning isn't everything, and competition will serve a useful function in society.

---

25. Frank Vascellaro, "'Just a Regular Guy from St. Paul': Frank Remembers Vince Flynn," CBS Minnesota, June 19, 2013, http://minnesota.cbslocal.com/2013/06/19/just-a-regular-guy-from-st-paul-frank-remembers-vince-flynn/.

Words of Wisdom for WOSPs

1. Provide balance for children. Sports aren't life, but they are meant to teach important life lessons.

2. Reinforce your children's interests and pay attention to their activities and the behaviors that reflect the values you want to instill in them.

3. Winning isn't everything. Focus on multiple outcomes and work to promote a growth mindset in your children. If they come to see hard work as a critical predictor of their success, they'll be far better off than those with a fixed mindset who believe talent trumps hard work and passion.

8

Busy as a Badge of Honor = Overscheduled Kids and Overstressed Parents

Over the last twenty years, I've noticed a distinct change in the response to the question, "How have you been?" Instead of responses like "great," "bad," or "fine," we often hear a simple four-letter word that's worn like a badge of honor, captures the tempo of our culture perfectly, and seems to justify our existence: *busy*. Our society has found ever-increasing ways to move faster and faster. Instead of making dinner, we eat at restaurants, and if those are too slow we eat at fast-food restaurants. If fast-food restaurants take too long, we go to drive-thrus, and if those take too long, we simply cook our meals in a microwave (or reheat fast food from the day before). We spend excessive amounts of money on high-speed Internet that's slowed down by antivirus software because our computers are exposed to nasty viruses while we surf countless websites at the speed of fiber optics. We want to communicate via email, Facebook, instant message, and text message, and then lament that we have no time to ourselves as our phone continues to buzz with every new Facebook friend, tweet from someone's Twitter feed, and text from an acquaintance updating us on their current location. We want fast cars, fast computers, fast phones, and fast food, and we want them all yesterday. And where has all of this speed and efficiency gotten us? B-U-S-Y.

What's the net result of all these time-saving conveniences? Surprisingly few of them actually save us time. Of course, part of the goal of these time-savers is to allow us more time to do the things we "really want to do." Which activities are we most passionate about in our lives? Based on many parents' behavior, one would conclude that we're passionate about watching five-year-olds playing youth soccer or T-ball, both of which feature on-field swarms that closely resembles ants at a picnic.

Imagine this scenario: Both parents work, and after a long (and *busy*) day, they text each other to see how their respective days went. Busy. Mom and Dad scurry to pick up their three kids. They rush home, change clothes, hurriedly cook dinner or grab a fast-food meal, check voicemail, tell the kids to hurry up because soccer starts in thirty minutes, find uniforms, finish eating, rush back to the car, speed to seven-year-old Billy's soccer game and five-year-old Jenny's T-ball game, while two-year-old Ian is left to watch. Billy's team is more interested in the popsicles after the game, while Jenny's game alternates between a wrestling match over the ball and a dandelion-picking contest in the outfield. Mercifully, the games end after an hour, the kids get their treats, and the family goes home, exhausted. The kids take quick baths, head to bed, and prepare to do it all over again tomorrow. So what exactly did these adorable children learn that evening? How to quickly get into and out of the car? How to eat dinner quickly? How to rush to get a uniform on? How to "play" a sport that is difficult for young children to play if they can't pass or dribble a soccer ball, or throw or catch a baseball? We probably hope they learned valuable lessons about sports, but it seems more likely that what they really learned was how to be *busy*.

I recently spoke to Mary, the sweet but stressed-out single mother of an eleven-year-old boy named Jason who attended my basketball camps for several years. When I asked her how she was doing, she gave the expected reply: busy. When I asked what she'd been busy doing, she said she'd recently taken a second job. She was working between sixty and seventy hours per week. When I commented on her ambitious drive, she dismissed the notion, saying simply, "I needed to make more money to pay for Jason's basketball team this summer."

I had a hard time believing what I was hearing, so I probed a bit more. She wanted Jason to be able to play on an AAU basketball team that traveled around the country during the summer. However, she didn't want Jason to travel alone with his team to Arkansas, Texas, Florida, and Las Vegas, so she felt she needed to travel with him. Money was already tight, and now she had bills for Jason's team, his shoes, his airfare, her airfare, hotel rooms, and so the decision was simple: She took a second job. Essentially, she was working twenty extra hours per week to pay for these extra expenses. She anticipated that she'd be spending more than $4,500 for his summer basketball experience. Not only that, she was missing out on valuable family time while she was working her second job. This example is merely the tip of the iceberg; stories abound of parents spending upwards of $30,000 per year to enroll their children in elite athletic academies.

David, the father of a camper, served as the vice president of a local traveling basketball organization. He also owns a very successful business. One afternoon, I asked him how his company was doing. His response was, "I hope my consulting company can run itself for the next couple months, because youth basketball has become a full-time job." Here's a successful businessman who was putting his company on hold to manage thirty to forty hours per week of phone calls, emails, practices, games, and scheduling for fifth-grade traveling basketball. As well intentioned as David may be, the stress of youth basketball was putting a significant strain on his company and his employees.

There's nothing inherently wrong with a parent making sacrifices for a child. Sacrificing for our children is admirable, and it's a responsibility shared by all parents. However, Mary and David exemplify a trend I believe is becoming all too common. Parents are sacrificing for causes that may or may not improve a child's life. Working twenty extra hours per week all spring so that the summer months can be consumed by traveling basketball around the country doesn't guarantee a better life for Jason, his mom, or their family. Months later, as Mary reflected back on those six months, the majority of her time was spent at her full-time job, her part-time job to earn money for basketball, or traveling to and watching basketball games. Is traveling for basketball or any other sport truly that important, or valuable enough in her son's life to justify this well-intentioned mom's investment of time and money? Will guiding his son's elementary-school basketball team result in a better life for David's son in the long term? Will his investment of time in youth sports help keep his company on a firm footing? If the answers to these questions aren't clear affirmatives, what drives parents like Mary and David?

Cognitive Dissonance

As described briefly at the start of Chapter 6, in the late 1950s, Leon Festinger proposed cognitive dissonance theory. Festinger defined dissonance as an uncomfortable psychological tension that arises from an inconsistency between our thoughts and actions. Festinger examined both the psychological consequences of an inconsistency between attitudes and behavior, as well as how people resolve this inconsistency. After all, we don't function well if we're in a perpetual state of discomfort, so we must do something to restore consistency between our attitudes and our behavior.

In his classic study on this topic, Festinger convinced college students to lie to a peer. Festinger first had students engage in an incredibly boring activity—rotating wooden pegs ninety degrees at a time for more than thirty minutes. By all accounts, it is as dull a task as one could perform. At the conclusion of the boring task, participants were told that the experiment was focused on how participants' expectations in motor activities affect their enjoyment of the activity. Participants were told they weren't given an expectation because they were in the neutral expectations condition. They were told that the next participant was in the positive expectation condition, but the other experimenter was ill. Participants were then asked to fill in for the sick experimenter by providing the participant in the waiting room with a positive expectation by telling him/her that the task they were going to do would be enjoyable. Essentially, participants were asked to lie.

Festinger's key variable in this study was how much participants were paid to lie. For serving as a substitute for the ill experimenter, one group of students was told they'd be paid one dollar while another group was told they'd be paid twenty dollars. All students proceeded to inform the next student the activity was quite enjoyable (a blatant lie). On their way out of the experiment, participants who had just told a lie for either a dollar or for twenty dollars were stopped by the actual experimenter and asked to rate their enjoyment of the activity.

Keep in mind that all participants presumably found this task as interesting as watching grass grow or paint dry. So who reported enjoying the task more, participants in the one-dollar group or participants in the twenty-dollar group? Most people predict the group paid twenty dollars would enjoy the boring activity more, because they would get a large sum of money (twenty dollars was a significant sum in the 1950s). To most people's surprise, however, individuals in the one-dollar group reported enjoying the activity more than individuals in the twenty-dollar group.

Why did the people paid a dollar enjoy this boring activity more than people paid twenty dollars? The answer to that question lies in the justification each group had to make to restore consistency between their attitudes and behavior. Let's put ourselves in each group's shoes for a moment. The group paid twenty dollars had sufficient justification for lying ("I was paid a lot of money. I lied, but only because I was paid a lot to do so."), and thus didn't have to change their attitude about the boring activity. However, the group paid only one dollar was stuck in a state of dissonance ("I believe in being honest. I was paid a measly dollar, and I know I wouldn't lie for a dollar. I'm a better person than that. Hmmm . . . actually, now that I think about it, I didn't lie. I actually found the task moderately interesting. It was kind of relaxing and once I got in a groove, I enjoyed myself."). By changing their attitudes about the activity, the one-dollar group had restored consistency between their attitudes and behavior. Of course, reducing dissonance in this manner is dangerous because it involves rationalization that allows us to ignore our hypocrisy, and thus increases the likelihood we'll continue a counterattitudinal behavior such as lying (or cheating or smoking) that opposes our beliefs. Put simply, humans are experts at rationalizing and trivializing counterattitudinal behavior.

Cognitive dissonance is a broad theory that explains a wide range of behavior. It helps explain why individuals who go through a severe initiation report liking a group more than those who do not—for example, members of sororities, fraternities, or the military. Cognitive dissonance gives us insight into how people justify their actions and effort. We can easily apply the theory to each of our lives in so many different arenas. All we need is an inconsistency between our attitudes and our behavior and dissonance is created. For example, if we spend inordinate amounts of time on work, exercise, reading, or relationships, we must justify those behaviors. The dangerous part of this phenomenon is that we're incredibly good at reducing our dissonance by changing our attitudes. In fact, we're so good at it that we often explain away our irrational and even immoral behavior by changing our attitudes.

College is noted for the amount of alcohol consumption that takes place. Consider the college freshman who never drank alcohol throughout high school and vowed to abstain through college. When he becomes homesick the first weekend of college, he attends a house party where he feels out of place because everyone else is drinking. Now imagine that after a couple of hours of being asked why he isn't drinking, he succumbs to peer pressure and has two beers. The next morning, what is his response? In all likelihood, he feels guilty, but rationalizes that it was "just a couple beers." However, two months later his drinking escalates, he has built up a tolerance, and now six beers is "just a few beers." In a matter of months, his attitude toward drinking has changed considerably due to his need to justify his actions. This can become a vicious cycle, where we justify increasing amounts of counterattitudinal behavior, until before we know it, we may discover that we've changed our values so they're more consistent with our behavior. So how does cognitive dissonance relate to youth sports and parents?

Dissonance in Youth Sports Parents: An Ongoing Cycle of Justifications

In understanding youth sports and parenting, cognitive dissonance provides insight into the tension parents experience watching their children play sports. Imagine Steve, a dad who simultaneously believes he ought to behave at youth sporting events but consistently yells at umpires at youth baseball games. According to Festinger, Steve will be in a state of cognitive dissonance whenever he screams at umpires, because his behavior is inconsistent with his attitudes. Furthermore, during this state of dissonance, Steve will feel like a hypocrite and should be highly motivated to reduce the inconsistency. However, the catch is that as much as most people want to behave consistently with their attitudes, once we have behaved inconsistently with them, it is hard to undo a behavior. It is far easier to change our attitudes and justify our behavior, and as we justify more and more, this process becomes easier and easier. This explains why initially smoking and drinking cause considerable dissonance, but after years and years, these behaviors create little, if any, dissonance.

In Steve's case, another parent suggested he should take it easy on the fifteen-year-old umpire. Steve's response: an obscene gesture, a nasty glare, and some choice words. The parent on the receiving end of this, a good friend of mine, was stunned. Not knowing what to do, he walked away, but not before Steve tried to confront him. How had

Steve alleviated his dissonance? In this case, Steve might justify his behavior by saying he wasn't that out of line, the umpire was terrible, the other parent was out of line, or simply that he's entitled to his own opinion. Whichever it may be, it's likely that Steve has alleviated the dissonance, restored consistency in his own mind, and convinced himself that his behavior was both justified and consistent with his beliefs.

Let's examine a very different type of situation that can produce the same type of tension in parents. Recall that our two basic social needs are to be liked and to be right. As a result, one of our basic tensions in life occurs anytime these two goals come in conflict. For instance, a college student might feel liked if she drinks, but believe that drinking is the wrong decision. In her mind then, either she chooses to fit in and make a poor decision (which she'll then justify) or make a good decision and feel left out (in which case she'll have to justify not being accepted). These basic social needs explain why parents often err by stroking their children's egos (see Chapter 3 on the need to feel good) or push their kids to be the next Tiger Woods (see Chapter 4 on the need to be good). Most of us find it challenging to live in a balanced manner, so we live in frequent states of dissonance.

Let's revisit our hardworking mother Mary, who took on an extra job to pay for her son's traveling team. Imagine that the first time Mary wanted to sign her son up for a basketball team, it was so expensive that she'd have had to take an additional part-time job to pay for the new sport. My hunch is that she would've thought this was over the top and refused to do so, even though she wants the best for her son. However, after years and years of investing time and money in his career, a large investment is much easier to justify. To put it simply, previous investments serve to justify subsequent investments, and this can become a vicious cycle that leads parents to be overinvolved, overworked, stressed, and frustrated.

The origins of this cycle originate in well-intentioned parents. As we look around at cases such as Tiger Woods and the Williams sisters, we realize the importance of giving children opportunities at a young age. Even if we have no delusions that our children will be professional athletes, we still believe that sports help foster the values of character, discipline, and teamwork. Thus, if starting sports at age six is good, starting at five is better. This is one of the reasons my friend Jim convinced me to enroll my son Jack in T-ball at age two. When he was four, I thought about what a great head start he'd have if he started basketball camp with kids who were seven to nine years of age. Although there may be nothing inherently wrong with providing these opportunities, if children aren't initially interested in an activity, the stage could be set for motivational problems down the road. The issue is that parents may have invested so much in their child's athletic career, they've lost sight of both the role of athletics and the goals of their child.

Fast-forward and imagine my son Jack has been playing traveling basketball for four years, and is now entering seventh grade. What if his team decides to play in tournaments every other weekend during the spring and summer? What if the varsity high school coach keeps track of who plays on the traveling team and who doesn't? What if Jack is pulled in different directions by basketball, baseball, soccer, and other hobbies? At this point a significant amount of time, money, and effort would have already been invested in Jack's career—plus Jack's own time and energy. Now imagine Jack feels pressured to play on the traveling team. So we decide to try the traveling team, despite the enormous investment of time and money.

Then, in the summer before he enters eighth grade, Jack's team decides to compete in three out-of-state tournaments, each of which requires flying to the tournament. He's young and should be supervised, so I decide to attend the tournaments. Just the cost of these three flights (for two passengers each) may be close to $3,000. This doesn't include hotel stays, meals, or all the other expenses of playing on a team. This vicious cycle could go on and on, and the dangerous part is that the more we invest in Jack's athletics, the more difficult it is to stop. In a way, it's reminiscent of Stanley Milgram's famous shock experiments. None of Milgram's participants would have shocked a stranger at 450 volts to start the experiment. However, starting at fifteen volts, and increasing in small increments of fifteen additional volts with each successive shock, provided participants with an opportunity for rationalization. Similarly, few parents would make an initial investment of several thousand dollars for youth sports. However, as time goes on, small investments of a few hundred dollars lead to larger ones of a few thousand dollars, and before we know it, several thousand dollars may seem reasonable, given all we've already invested. Typically, this perpetual cycle of spending money and investing time will continue until one of two things happen—kids get cut or they quit.

Cutdown Day

For years in Major League Baseball, when a player was being released from the team, he would find a little colored sticker in his locker that signified, "Go see the manager—your days here are done." Although he might enter the manager's office with a glimmer of hope, he knew in his heart that he was headed for the minor leagues. One of the greatest challenges about athletics is that at some point, we're all faced with the reality that we aren't good enough. This is true in individual drills performed each day in practice, in games, and in every athlete's career. Regardless of whether it's getting cut from the A traveling team in eighth grade, not making the high school varsity baseball team, getting cut by one's college team, or a ten-year NFL veteran being released, we're all going to be told we're "not good enough" at some time. In fact, this may be tougher for the professional athlete to cope with because sports have been such an integral part of the athlete's self-concept for his or her entire life. When children and parents have invested enormous amounts of time and money in an activity, being told one isn't good enough can be quite disheartening. In fact, this is when parents often model behaviors for their children about handling adversity and coping with defeat.

When children are cut from a team, they learn powerful messages both from the negative feedback of being cut and from the reactions of their parents. Does the parent immediately blame the coach? Imagine what goes through a disappointed child when a parent says about the coach: "He's an idiot. You were the best player at tryouts and deserved to make the team. I'm going to call him and let him know." Now, the child may have deserved to make it, but I doubt the coach believes this to be the case. I've yet to meet a coach who would cut the best player on the team for no reason. Coaches make lots of mistakes, but I haven't run across any who want to cut their top players.

What does this type of parental response teach the child? It teaches him or her to blame others when things go wrong. This type of self-serving bias teaches children to take responsibility for successes and blame others for failures. Unfortunately, this seems antithetical to the tenets of sports, which teach humility after a victory and resilience after a defeat. Dissonance occurs when a parent thinks, "We didn't spend all this money for nothing! He deserves to be on the team!" The insinuation is that in order to justify previous expenses, "my child must continue to play." The result is often a parent lashing out at the coach or the child out of frustration that the time and money invested now appears to have gone down the drain.

Neal Anderson is one of the best pure shooters I have ever seen. In 2004, he set the single-season record for the most three-point shots made at the University of St. Thomas. To give you an idea of how automatic his shot was, one day after practice, Neal made fifty-two three-pointers in a row! He simply didn't miss when he was open. Neal's high school career was a different story. In tenth grade, Neal got cut from the tenth-grade team. In eleventh grade, Neal got cut from the junior varsity. In twelfth grade, Neal got cut from the varsity. For three straight years Neal was told he wasn't good enough to be on the sophomore team, the junior varsity, or the varsity.

Neal moved on to the University of St. Thomas, where he sang in the choir, majored in business, and played intramural basketball. After two intramural seasons, several of our players told me about this young man who they believed was a better shooter than anyone we had on the team. Neal tried out, made the team, and over the next three years, made the varsity, became a starter, was named a captain, and then voted an All-Conference player.

Had Neal's parents, Jim and Phoebe, told him how badly he'd been mistreated in high school, Neal likely would have stopped working at basketball. He'd have believed that he was being treated unfairly and that it wasn't worth his time to continue playing. Instead, Neal's parents simply encouraged him to pursue his passions. Basketball happened to be one of these passions. Neal spent time in the gym, never complained about being cut, and simply outworked all those players who made the team ahead of him in high school. Not surprisingly, Neal Anderson is not only a great shooter, but an even better person. His parents' responses to Neal being cut taught him valuable lessons about persistence, staying positive, and following one's dreams.

Earlier, I also mentioned Tommy Hannon, who had attended several of my basketball camps when he was in grade school. Tommy didn't take great care of himself, and by the time he was a junior in high school, he'd ballooned up to 255 pounds. He was cut from his high school basketball program (both varsity and junior varsity, which isn't easy to do). Tommy had a choice to make—either blame the coaches or get to work.

Tommy's two best friends, John Nance (who earned a football scholarship to the University of Minnesota before transferring to star in basketball at St. Thomas) and Michael Floyd (a future All-American receiver at Notre Dame and NFL player for the Arizona Cardinals), told him, "Tommy, we're really athletic and hardworking . . . you're neither!" Tommy looked in the mirror and didn't like what he saw. He lost nearly fifty pounds in one year, worked incredibly hard, and he made the junior varsity as a senior (not a great accomplishment). He began carrying a picture of himself in his wallet to remind him of the most out of shape he had been.

He played so well in junior varsity that he was moved up to the varsity and was the sixth man on his high school varsity by the end of the season. He'd now grown to six-foot-six and we began recruiting him. He enrolled at the University of St. Thomas, played on our junior varsity as a freshman, before making our varsity as a sophomore. By the end of the year, he was playing as much as any of our post players. The next season, Tommy started every game for us, we won the Division III National Championship, and Tommy was named to the All Final Four team. In a mere four years, Tommy went from not playing organized basketball to starring on a national championship team, in large part due to his persistence and willingness to recognize and address his shortcomings. Tommy went on to captain another Final

Four team his senior year, was named an All-American, graduated with honors as a finance major, played professional basketball in Australia, and now works in finance in the Twin Cities. Tommy embodies the competitive spirit and desire to work on one's weaknesses that we hope athletics teach our children. To this day, Tommy carries that picture of himself as a junior in high school to remind himself that there's no substitute for hard work.

Quitting

As discussed in Chapter 6, many children suffer from burnout and quit sports. How paradoxical it seems that children who initially love a game find their passion sapped by powerful environmental forces that dampen their motivation. This can be equally frustrating for the overinvolved parent. The tension lies in a chain of events that is marked by (a) a child feeling pressure to play, (b) the child feeling as if the costs of playing outweigh the benefits, and (c) parents who believe the investment in sports requires continuation of an activity. This chain of events typically ends badly with a child either quitting, or continuing to play simply to please his or her parents. In either case, the decreased motivation, accompanied by a strained relationship with one's parents, will be challenging for a child to manage.

Many high school athletes stop playing at some point because they feel the rewards don't match the costs. Maybe they want more time to study, more time with friends, more time to work. None of these is necessarily a bad reason to stop playing sports. In fact, for many adolescents, this is the natural progression of events. Many large high schools have three basketball teams for freshmen (forty-five freshman play), one team for sophomores (fifteen sophomores play), and a varsity team comprised mainly of juniors and seniors. Of that group, maybe two to four seniors will start. If we rewind, we would find that more than one hundred kids were playing basketball for these schools in first grade, and 2 to 4 percent of them went on to start for their varsity team. Clearly, not everyone can make varsity, so the harsh reality is that some kids may choose not to play before they get cut. Although painful, this can be a mature decision if parents serve as a sounding board for children, but don't pressure them one way or the other. After all, kids need to learn to make decisions for themselves, and there's nothing that says all kids have to play high school sports (in fact, from a numbers perspective, not all can).

As a college professor, one of my roles is to serve as an academic advisor to approximately thirty-five students each semester. Over the course of a few years, I get to know a fair amount about students' lives beyond academics—their families, their hobbies, and how they've changed over time. I'm often struck by how often students who were passionate about athletics during high school not only give up their sport in college, but also give up working out altogether. Not playing a sport in college is understandable. Students may choose not to play based on their chances of making the team, interests in other activities, a focus on academics, or a loss of interest in the sport. However, one of the presumed benefits of athletic participation is better health and fitness. We would hope that the goal of a healthy lifestyle wouldn't disappear simply because the student is no longer part of organized sports. However, I'm no longer surprised when students tell me they've lost motivation to work out because they don't have anything to work out for. It is as if one's health and well-being aren't sufficient motivators to exercise!

Certainly, many students exercise regularly. For others, it takes putting on the "freshman fifteen" to realize that working out is an important part of a healthy lifestyle. From a motivational perspective, it's interesting to note that this lack of motivation appears to be caused, in part, by athletic participation at a younger age. Recall the overjustification effect described in Chapter 6. Numerous studies have shown that when individuals are rewarded for participating in an activity they already enjoy, subsequent intrinsic motivation decreases. This is one explanation for what happens when these students get to college—without the extrinsic motivator of being on a team, winning, and gaining prestige and status, exercise begins to seem pointless to some students.

What to Do with the Investment?

With forty-one million kids in youth sports, we know many of them will stop participating at some point. When parents have invested a tremendous amount of time and energy, the end of a child's athletic participation may put a wedge in the parent-child relationship. If parents feel as if their investment was wasted, they may pressure their children to continue playing, even against a child's wishes. To use a business term, the parents still expect a solid return on investment.

Nikki Arola, a former student of mine who's now working on her Ph.D. in clinical psychology, and I conducted a study to examine what parents expect from youth athletics. We provided parents with different scenarios that varied how much playing time their child received, how much time and money they invested in their child's athletic career, and whether or not their child learned valuable lessons through sports. We measured parental satisfaction with their child's experience in sports and found that when parents invested a lot of time and money in their child's career, playing time had a significant effect on their satisfaction whereas whether or not their child learned important life lessons did not. Sadly, we found clear evidence that playing time trumped learning when it came to youth sports.

There seems to be one reasonable way to avoid this state of cognitive dissonance when a child stops playing: reframe the *return* portion of the return on investment. Instead of expecting a return in terms of playing time, winning, or a college scholarship, parents ought to expect sports to provide valuable lessons on teamwork, competition, cooperation, setting goals, unselfishness, and character development. Then, if a child decides to stop participating, but has developed these valuable skills and learned these important lessons, parents should feel exceptionally good about their investment.

Furthermore, if the goal is character development, children are far less likely to feel pressure from parents to participate, excel, and win, and thus their intrinsic motivation will drive their goals and experience. Taken together, this balance should prevent dissonance, which proves to be such a dangerous cycle for parents and children in youth sports. In sum, parents need to be more intentional about what the goals are, and what needs to be done to achieve them. For example, spending thousands of dollars, taking on a second job, traveling all over the country, and spending every weekend in a gym don't seem like requirements for teaching a child important life skills. Too often, we forget that these skills can be learned through informal play and in venues other than athletic fields and courts. These skills can be learned in the classroom, at home doing chores, or by volunteering in one's neighborhood.

Most of us have had our sports careers end at some point.

Although the end may have been difficult, the reality is that sports will forever be etched in our person in terms of the lessons we learned, the way athletics shaped our characters, and the friendships we formed. As busy as our lives and our children's lives are, it's our job to ensure that our children have a broad range of rewarding experiences. Living a balanced life is difficult in our culture. Modeling balance in our own lives and avoiding overscheduling and putting pressure on our children will go a long way toward providing a balanced perspective on life for our children.

Words of Wisdom for WOSPs

1. Be intentional with goals for children. Overscheduling can lead to increased investments of time and money that are difficult to decrease in the future. Dan Neuhart, author of *If You Had Controlling Parents* (1998), puts it well: "Overinvolvement reflects some emotional need on the parent's part, not the best interest of the child."[26]

2. Accept that some outcomes of sports will be difficult, frustrating, and painful. Seek to understand how your child is experiencing these tough times, and encourage them to grow and learn from adversity.

---

26. Stephanie Dunnewind, "When Parents Are Too Hands On," *Seattle Times*, September 4, 2004, http://community.seattletimes.nwsource.com/archive/?date=2 0040904&slug=involvedparents04.

3. Beware of cognitive dissonance that can occur from escalating investments in youth sports. The more we invest, the more likely we will be to invest even more in the future. This cycle can get out of control quickly if we don't monitor it.

9

Finding the Balance of Excellence

For centuries, philosophers have espoused the importance of balance in life. For just as long, humans have struggled to attain it. Of course, balance can ebb and flow in life as we adjust to new challenges, stressors, and opportunities. One could have a seemingly balanced life, but then experience a job change or an illness, or be blessed with a newborn, and undoubtedly balance is out the window, at least for a time. Life happens, and balance is a subjective and moving target.

Many of the topics covered so far directly connect to the challenge of leading a balanced life. For example, focusing on our two basic social needs, the need to be liked and the need to be right, and the dissonance that follows when these needs are in conflict. Much of the stress WOSPs experience stems from wanting their kids to be liked and feel good, while at the same time, wanting their children to excel. How can parents strike a healthy balance when it comes to their own lives and the lives of their children, particularly when it comes to youth sports?

"Congratulations, You Lead a Balanced Life." Curse or Compliment?

My high school gave the Ray Lepsche Award to a sophomore boy at the end of each school year. As I recall, the award was accompanied by a plaque and moderate scholarship. None of us knew who Ray Lepsche was, but I vividly remember the assembly in which it was awarded because it was the first time that I was scared to death I might win an award. Why? The teacher presenting the award provided some background on the award's namesake before introducing the recipient of the award. The teacher described Lepsche as an average student, who worked hard but didn't get strong grades. Furthermore, he was described as a nice, quiet kid who wasn't an overly popular student. Finally, the teacher discussed Lepsche's athletic prowess, or lack thereof. He played sports, but not very well. By the end of the speech, all of us sophomore boys were slumped in our chairs, praying we wouldn't be saddled with what had become infamously known as the Mr. Average award. Throughout the gymnasium, voices whispered about who might win the award.

My prayers were answered, but a friend's weren't. My friend Dave received the Mr. Average award. Let me tell you a bit more about Dave and you'll quickly see he was anything but average. Dave was an honors student, earned nearly straight As, and was in the top 5 to 10 percent of our class. Dave was in all the honors classes and worked very hard. Socially, Dave was the kind of guy everyone liked and got along with during school. While not the most popular guy in the school, he was certainly well liked and respected by his peers and teachers. What about athletics? Dave played three sports: football, basketball, and track (he was a high jumper). By the time Dave was a senior, he'd played in the state tournament in football, been a member of a state-championship team in basketball, and qualified for the state track and field meet in the high jump.

If you're thinking that Dave hardly sounds like an average high school student, you're right. Two years later, a group of us were recounting Dave's award, and we took a count of all the males in our class who were top 10 percent in the class, popular, and a member of three varsity sports. How many were there? Dave was the only one. That's right—the Mr. Average award went to a truly outstanding and special student. Now it was true to say Dave may not have been the brightest, or the most popular, or the most athletic, but in terms of balance, he certainly blazed a trail of which any high school student could be proud. However, in our culture, balance is often viewed as being average across the board, rather than as a "balance of excellence." This is one of the reasons I believe many parents err to an extreme of either helping their child feel good (Chapter 3) or helping their child excel (Chapter 4). The danger is that pursuing one of these goals without the other can lead to imbalances in a child's experience, which often translate to problems later on in life.

Why is balance so difficult? Even though virtually all of us espouse balance as an important part of our lives, few of us perceive that we've attained it. I believe there are three major reasons why a balanced life is so difficult to master, and each of these reasons is evident in the world of youth sports.

More Is Better

Our culture is built on individualism. From the time we're young, we're told that if we want something badly enough, and if we work hard enough for it, we can attain it. Along with this individualism comes a strong desire for achievement. Typically, achievement is measured in a linear fashion. Simply put, more is better. If having a fifteen-hundred-square-foot house is good, a two-thousand-square-foot house is better. If making $50,000 per year is good, making $75,000 is better. Quite simply, if some is good, more is better.

In his 1988 book *Show Time*, legendary Los Angeles Lakers coach Pat Riley described what he calls the Disease of More. Specifically, Riley suggests that champions from a previous season typically struggle the next year because every player wants more than the year before. They want more playing time, more shots, more points, and more money. It's virtually impossible for all players to accomplish these goals because there are a finite number of minutes, shots, and points to go around. In fact, players can end up competing with their teammates to meet these goals, while simultaneously forgetting their ultimate goal is to work together toward a common goal. The "more is better" mindset can damage teams and lead to a host of problems.

Each summer, SuperAmerica typically has a Big Gulp special that advertises any size soft drink for only sixty-nine cents. In a "more is better" society, it would be hard to justify purchasing anything less than the 44 oz. Super Big Gulp. I have been in SuperAmerica, purchased a 20 oz. soda (because that's all I wanted), and had the clerk ask me if I knew I could get any size for the same price. When I acknowledge that I know that, the clerk typically looks at me quizzically, as if I don't understand basic logic. A couple times, to preserve my image at SuperAmerica, I've even agreed with the clerk and gone to get a 44 oz. cup instead. Several hours later, when I feel nauseated because I consumed more than a quart of Cherry Slurpee, I wonder why I was so easily convinced to behave counter to my attitudes. Part of the explanation lies in cognitive dissonance theory. How could I justify choosing a 20 oz. beverage for the same price as a 44 oz. beverage, even though I didn't want double the caffeine and sugar? Amazingly, 8 to 12 oz. beverages were the norm several decades ago. This more-is-better trend isn't limited to convenience stores, but plays itself out regularly in the world of youth sports as well.

Consider the parent who decides he wants his daughter to be as good as she can be in softball after her first season in the sport goes well. Instead of signing her up for one softball team, he signs her up for three teams. She also has an individual hitting coach, attends a speed/quickness training facility, and lifts weights for four days per week with her new gym membership. Considered separately, none of these decisions is wrong. The question parents are confronted with is if some training is good, is more always better? Is there a point not only of diminishing returns, but of negative returns? At what point will young athletes burn out, feel as if their entire identity is wrapped up in sports, or decide their parents are trying to control their existence? At what point does the escalation of commitment by children and parents in youth sports set up a house of cards doomed to fall and destined to fail? Our more-is-better culture makes it difficult to be balanced because once we set a goal, it's hard to just be decent, lest we win some version of the dreaded Mr. Average award. This doesn't mean we ought to encourage mediocrity, but rather that as parents we keep in mind that not every child can be the best, or even above average. Combine that with parents' desire to provide their children with opportunities and the enticing high-profile success stories of childhood prodigies, and it's easy to see how parents get caught in the belief that more is better.

Winning Isn't Everything, It's the Only Thing: The Drive to Be Number One

It is quite common to hear a newly hired coach open his first press conference by saying the goal is to win championships. In the same way that few of us want to be average, there's nothing wrong with this goal of winning titles. People who work in competitive industries typically want to be the best. However, our culture has taken being number one to a level that can be considered both irrational and extrinsic in focus.

By definition, competition is a zero-sum event in which one person (or team) wins and one person (or team) loses. Thus, 50 percent of the time, competitors will walk away beaten. Valuable lessons can be learned from a loss. However, if the sole goal is to win, then half the time competitors walk away abject failures.

Vince Lombardi, the renowned coach of the Super Bowl Champion Green Bay Packers became famous for the line: "Winning isn't everything, it's the only thing." Over several decades, this mindset has become a badge of honor for many competitors. The danger of this notion is that it justifies virtually any action performed in the service of victory. However, the oft-quoted line is very different from what Lombardi actually said: "Winning isn't everything but the desire to win is the only thing."[27] The actual quote places a premium on effort, but our society has bought into the idea that performance is solely defined by its outcome.

This emphasis on being the best in our society brings out both the best and worst in people. For example, watching Michael Phelps in the 2008 Olympics was nothing short of inspirational. Phelps broke Mark

---

27. John Maxymuk, *Packers by the Numbers: Jersey Numbers and the Players Who Wore Them* (Boulder, CO: Prairie Oak Press, 2003), 28.

Spitz's record for gold medals in a single Olympiad by winning eight gold medals. Phelps won one of those races by one hundredth of a second in a heroic comeback. If Phelps had swam two hundredths of a second slower and won only seven gold medals instead of eight, would he have failed? Expectations were so high for Phelps that many would have felt he'd failed (or even choked) had he not won all eight golds in Beijing. The reality is that his performance was one for the ages, but it would have been significantly diminished had he won seven golds and one silver. In 2012, as soon as Phelps took fourth in a race, critics were quick to note how he'd fallen from grace (even though he still won more medals in 2012 than any other swimmer!).

Growing up as a fan of the Minnesota Vikings, who've lost in all four of their Super Bowl appearances, I learned quickly to expect the worst. Although their performance in the Super Bowl left a lot to be desired, it was as if they'd failed more miserably than 90 percent of the NFL teams that have never been to four Super Bowls. Rarely do we remember the runners-up in life, even though the difference between first and second is frequently infinitesimal, particularly when we're talking about first and second in the world at a given sport.

How does this desire to be number one play out in youth sports? First, parents want their children to be the best. This desire is natural, and every parent has experienced that rush of pride after watching a son or daughter accomplish something spectacular. The problem is that parents can quickly transform this pride into heightened and unrealistic expectations for their children. These expectations can create pressure for children, who in turn may become burned out, lose motivation, and eventually disengage.

The media's emphasis on being number one is legendary. I recall being in eighth grade in 1987, when *Sports Illustrated* published the top basketball player in each grade, all the way down to the sixth grade! Some of the high school players in the rankings went on to NBA careers (Kenny Anderson and Alonzo Mourning), while the younger kids (Michael Irvin, Brian Crowe, and Barnabas James) were never heard from on the national scene. Amazingly, I still recall where I was when I saw that issue of *Sports Illustrated*, and how disappointed I felt that I wasn't featured (though I was hardly the best eighth grader on my own team!). I don't recall wondering how in the world *Sports Illustrated* knew all of the sixth-, seventh-, and eighth-grade basketball players in the country. Today, you can find long lists of rankings of fifth and sixth graders, and you could even enter your second grader-to-be in the AAU national tournament held in Memphis.

While it may have been a bit disheartening that I wasn't featured in magazines in eighth grade, today I worry more about the youngsters who were profiled. After all, if the goal is to be number one, and a child reaches that goal by the sixth grade, what's left to accomplish? What happens to their work ethic? Do they stop focusing on improvement and become afraid to fail, more worried about losing their number-one ranking than about becoming better athletes? Do they become arrogant? Do they expect the world to cater to them from here on out? How and why would it be important or useful, or even possible, to rank children at that age?

When parents decide the sole goal is for their child to be a number, it places the more noble goals of youth sports in the backseat. In the same way a simplified version of Vince Lombardi's quote has been used as a justification for any act that leads to a victory, highlighting kids may lead to a justification of virtually any behavior that increases the likelihood of a number-one ranking for a team or an individual. Sadly, if all our children learn from sports is a burning desire to be number one at all costs, then we should expect to have more scandals like those we've seen in corporate America in recent years, for example on Wall Street during the economic downturn. Consider the executives at Enron in the 1990s who were simply trying to win on a much larger stage than that of youth sports, but undoubtedly, their competitive drive and win-at-all-costs mentality had been reinforced along the way. Before they knew it, their desire to win obscured their professed values and allegiance to shareholders and they had dug a hole that kept getting deeper and deeper with justifications.

How Do We Quantify Balance?

While "more is better" and "number one at all costs" mindsets present challenges to a balanced lifestyle, they can certainly be overcome with practice. Over time, individuals can begin to realize that enough is enough, and that winning is truly not everything. However, a third challenge to balance may be more difficult to conquer—that is, how does one measure whether or not balance has been achieved?

One of the more consistent findings in the field of psychology is that goals are good. This will likely strike you as self-evident. In 1990, psychologists Edwin A. Locke and Gary P. Latham published a classic work summarizing the effects of goals. Quite simply, their results provide unequivocal evidence that having a goal is better than not having a goal.[28] Now, there are all sorts of ways we can compare different types of goals to see which are most effective. Mastery versus performance? Self-set versus assigned? Specific versus vague? Measurable versus not measurable? The list goes on and on. The key point for us is that goals are good. Why? Goals guide and direct our behavior. Goals

---

28. Edwin A. Locke, et al., *A Theory of Goal Setting & Task Performance* (Upper Saddle River, NJ: Prentice Hall, 1990).

are like a buoy at sea, providing us clear and immediate feedback if we get off course. As a result, it's easy to see why we develop more-is-better thinking—because it's consistent with goal-setting theory and is effective in many areas of life.

On the other hand, measuring balance is difficult. Does a balanced life refer to being average in all areas? If so, we may find many people will change their minds about a desire to be balanced. The reality is most people are hired for a job not because they're average in all areas, but because they have a special skill set that differentiates them from other candidates.

Does balance refer to excellence across the board? It may, but this isn't an attainable goal for many people. After all, despite the message in the 1998 movie *Pleasantville*, we all simply cannot be above average.

If someone aspires to be balanced, does that mean they'll be good at parenting, work, hobbies, and recreational activities? Balance is difficult to measure precisely because each of us has different goals and priorities. For one person, balance may mean excellence as a parent and as an employee—and that's all.

For another individual, balance may mean some degree of competence as a student, athlete, choir member, friend, and employee. Due to our different goals, balance will require a different yardstick for everyone. As a result, most of us focus on those things that can be measured more easily, which are (a) can I get more of a good thing, and (b) am I number one?

Taken together, these three challenges to balance lead young athletes (and their parents) to place an extreme emphasis on doing more, even if it crosses the line. More is better seems OK when it means improving one's free-throw percentage. However, in most things, there's a palpable law of diminishing returns. I used to ask the hardest worker I've ever coached, Bryan Schnettler, how much more he could practice shooting. He was one of the top three-point shooters in the nation. Each day, he'd spend two hours outside of practice in the gym perfecting his shot. It worked, and in only three years at St. Thomas, he shattered every school and conference three-point record. However, at a certain point, he wasn't going to see his shooting improve as much as other areas of his game. His senior year he decided to work more on other areas of his game, such as ball-handling, defense, and finding other ways to get shots off. Bryan became a more complete player and finished his career as an All-American guard. One year later, Bryan was coaching high school basketball and remarked how much he wished he could play one more year, so he could use his newfound perspective as a coach to implement a more well-rounded approach to his training.

The more-is-better virus can also invade parents' thinking about the number of sports, teams, camps, and personal trainers a young athlete ought to have. These can result in athlete burnout, overtraining, physical fatigue, staleness, and frustration on the part of both parent and child. At a certain point, enough is simply enough. Of course, the second challenge to a balanced life—the drive to be number one— justifies virtually any action in the more-is-better way of thinking. This drive to be number one is an extrinsic focus that is dangerous for both motivation and performance. If a child comes to believe the only value of working hard is to be number one, the vast majority of children will feel like failures and give up once being number one becomes unattainable. Finally, although parents may want their child to be happy, healthy, and lead a balanced life, the difficulty in measuring balance makes it easier for parents to simply rely on more specific, objective measures of how children are doing. In the end, these challenges to balance help explain why we see younger and younger athletes specializing in a specific sport, and why their primary goal becomes being number one, or another goal such as obtaining a college scholarship (also a measurable outcome).

Although it's difficult to pursue or even quantify balance, there is evidence that a balanced approach to life may be more adaptive than black-or-white, either-or solutions. Let's consider examples from three distinct areas of research: achievement goals and academics, competition and cooperation in athletics, and parental styles in raising children.

Achievement Goals in College Classes

When I ask college students their goals at the outset of classes that I teach, invariably they respond "get a good grade." Now a good grade for one student may be an A while for another student, it may be a B. The key point is that students appear oriented to succeed in terms of their performance. *Performance goals*, defined as the desire to demonstrate competence, orient students toward certain behaviors and study strategies they hope will enable them to attain their goal of performing well in a class. Shortly after discussing the weight they attach to grades, students typically report wanting to learn and develop their skills in a discipline class. This desire to demonstrate competence is referred to as a *mastery goal*.

Finally, some students will readily acknowledge that they hope not to expend much effort in my class. I'm always a bit perplexed that students would be willing to pay so much money for school and spend so many years there, yet hope to do as little work as possible—and that students are willing to share this unflattering information about their work habits with their professor. These goals, referred to as *work-avoidance goals*, involve a desire to do as little work as possible.

Early research by social psychologist Carol S. Dweck and her colleagues found that when students were given a mastery goal, they were more motivated than those who were given a performance goal. The majority of Dweck's research was conducted with children. She developed a model that highlighted the beneficial role of a mastery mindset because it promotes a willingness to take risks, the ability to perceive failure as a challenge, and a focus on controlling what one can control—namely one's own actions.

While Dweck has published a number of studies that demonstrate these positive effects of mastery goals, it's important to note that these studies have typically assigned students to either a mastery or a performance goal. That means students weren't able to endorse both goals, which runs counter to the anecdotal evidence I encounter when students say they want to perform well and learn a lot in class. For the better part of a decade, Judith Harackiewicz (my graduate-school advisor), several of my former grad-school colleagues, and I examined the possibility that students could adopt both mastery goals (a desire to develop competence) and performance goals (a desire to demonstrate competence).

Rather than proposing an either-or, more-is-better approach to mastery goals, we have allowed students to tell us what their goals are in college classes. So, students can report that they're highly, moderately, or not at all mastery oriented. Similarly, they can report that they are highly, moderately, or not at all performance oriented. Under this framework, a student who cared a lot about learning and not so much about grades would be high on mastery goals and low on performance goals. On the other hand, a student motivated solely by grades would be high on performance goals and low on mastery goals. Because mastery and performance goals are relatively independent constructs, we also considered the possibility that a student can be high on both mastery and performance goals. This student would place a great deal of importance on both learning and grades.

In study after study with college students, we have found similar results: Students who adopt mastery goals report being more interested in their psychology classes. However, to the surprise of many, we haven't found that mastery goals predict grades in college classes. As educators, this is somewhat disheartening because we would hope that those students who strive to learn the most would also receive better grades. They do not. Thus, the students who adopt the goal of learning end up finding the course material more interesting, but they didn't perform better in the class.

Students who adopt performance goals don't report higher (or lower) levels of interest or enjoyment than students who don't adopt performance goals. However, students who adopt performance goals do perform better in class than those students who don't adopt them. We observed that students who strive to do well in class perform better. These findings were a bit controversial because they contradicted goal theories that argued mastery goals are superior to performance goals. Our results led us to promote a multiple-goals approach in which students adopt both mastery and performance goals. A student who chooses both mastery and performance goals has the best chance of being interested in the material, enjoying class, and performing well in class. This is an example of a situation in which a balanced approach is more effective than an either-or, black-or-white solution.

As an aside, students who adopted work-avoidance goals were less interested, enjoyed the class less, and performed more poorly. Taking into consideration all of our observations, we recommend college students adopt both mastery and performance goals, and stay away from work-avoidance goals. There is something to be gained from both mastery and performance goals, and little to be gained from avoiding work.

Cooperation versus Competition

For decades, researchers have debated the merits of competition and cooperation. Many have advocated for cooperation because it can create group harmony, increase performance, and reduce pressure. On the other hand, competition can provide an exciting challenge. It's a debate that may not have a simple answer. Instead, the solution probably lies not in one extreme or the other, but rather in a balance, or blend, of cooperation and competition.

Many of the activities people engage in combine cooperation and competition. Whether it is softball, soccer, basketball, baseball, or flag football, many of our recreational activities involve a blend of these two apparently opposite forces. Several years ago, I was struggling to formulate a dissertation thesis to complete my doctorate at the University of Wisconsin–Madison. For four years, I had studied the effects of competition on intrinsic motivation. I didn't feel capable of conjuring new, novel, creative ideas. On a sunny July evening, I went for a bike ride through Elver Park in Madison. As I cruised through the park, I biked past a pickup basketball game, then a co-ed softball game, and finally a youth girls' soccer match.

Suddenly, an idea hit me. For years, I'd understood that something drew people (including me) to competition. However, in many laboratory studies, researchers have found that competition undermined intrinsic motivation, particularly for individuals low in achievement motivation. Most lab studies were individual competitions, pitting one psychology student against another in a relatively sterile environment, doing an activity in which neither of them was very invested. Maybe the key was to combine the thrill of competition with the benefits of working with a group toward a common goal. This would allow people to (a) not feel entirely responsible for a loss, and (b) share the communal benefits of working together as a group.

Surprisingly little research has examined the effects of combining cooperation and competition, with most research focused purely on whether cooperation or competition is more positive. To address this, Judith Harackiewicz and I conducted a series of studies at my youth basketball camps. Our hypothesis was that both cooperation and competition have unique features that people may find enjoyable. Thus, we predicted a combination of cooperation and competition (intergroup competition) would provide the best of both worlds.

Participants were pretested on their free-throw shooting to assess their baseline ability levels. We then asked participants in our studies to shoot ten free throws under one of several sets of instructions.

Pure competition: Some campers were paired with one other camper (of equal ability) and told to try to make more free throws out of ten than their opponent.

Pure cooperation: Some campers were paired with one other camper (of equal ability) and told to try to make a certain number of free throws out of twenty. Their shared goal was based on their pretest performance. So, if each camper of the pair had made seven out of ten the first day of camp, their dual goal would be fifteen out of twenty.

Intergroup competition: Some campers were paired with one other camper (of equal ability) and told to try to make more free throws out of twenty than their opponents, a separate pair of campers (of equal ability to each other and their opponents).

After completing their free throws, campers were given feedback on whether they (or their team) had won the competition (or met their goal). Campers were then asked to complete a questionnaire that assessed their enjoyment of the activity.

Across four studies where we combined cooperation and competition, our results were as clear and consistent as any results I've obtained in any studies I've conducted over the past sixteen years. Participants enjoyed shooting free throws more in the intergroup competition condition compared to pure cooperation or pure competition. In addition, in two of three studies where we measured performance, participants in the intergroup-competition condition performed better than participants in the pure-cooperation or pure-competition conditions. Indeed, it appears that there is something beneficial about both cooperation and competition, and by combining them, participants experienced the best of both worlds.

Why Is Intergroup Competition Positive?

One explanation for these results was that the intergroup-competition condition was simply more social, and that's why participants enjoyed it more than pure cooperation or pure competition. In the intergroup-competition condition, there were four participants, whereas the other two conditions included just two each. To address this possibility, in our final study, we included a four-person cooperation condition. Once again, participants in the intergroup competition enjoyed the activity more than those engaging in the four-person cooperation condition, indicating that the number of people was not the driving factor.

Here's another example of the importance of balance. A combination of two variables—such as cooperation and competition, and mastery and performance goals—proves more beneficial than one or the other.

Parenting Styles

One of my good friends grew up as the youngest child in a family of thirteen children. He tells the story of the first time he ever asked his father "why?" in response to a request (or demand) his father made to perform a household task. "WHAPPPP!" went the back of the dad's hand across the boy's face. As my friend says, "We learned quickly at our house not to ask questions. When we were told to do something, we did it. Although we learned obedience to authority, we didn't learn to be as curious or creative as we might have had questions been encouraged."

Contrast that stinging example with a former student of mine. He was allowed to do whatever he wanted, whenever he wanted, throughout his childhood. His parents gave him unlimited reign and he took it. By the time he was eighteen, he'd been in trouble for alcohol and drug use. He was very bright, but struggled with self-discipline and work ethic. It was as if he knew the right thing to do, but it was difficult for him to turn away from immediate temptation. If he had a choice between studying and partying, it was a no-brainer for him.

The first story depicts an authoritarian parent, in a family that seems like a dictatorship to the children. There are clear (often strict) rules, severe consequences, no time for discussion, and little in the way of nurturing behavior. The second story depicts a permissive parent who offers few rules or guidelines and a fair amount of support and nurturing. Now, the outcome of those two stories could flip. There are plenty of examples of children who are raised in an authoritarian home who go wild when they get to college and the rules are relaxed. Similarly, some children raised in permissive families crave discipline and rules, and find a mentor who provides this structure for them.

So which parenting style is better, authoritarian or permissive? Actually, neither parenting style is ideal. Each has a glaring weakness. The authoritarian style provides discipline and the permissive style provides support and nurturing, but each is lacking a critical element. Research studies have consistently demonstrated that a third parenting style, the authoritative parent, leads to numerous benefits for children, including higher self-esteem, mental health, independence, achievement, and social skills.

Once again we see the value of balance. In this case, parents who combine love and support with discipline and structure appear to create the optimal environment for children. This is an environment where children know they're loved unconditionally, yet where they're also held to standards, with consequences for poor behavior. The authoritative household typically has clear rules, clear consequences, and the children have a voice in some part of the rules. As a result, children feel heard, valued, and respected.

In a study at my basketball camp, Sara Padley, a former undergraduate student of mine, and I asked children to report the parenting styles of their mothers and fathers. Parents could range from low to moderate to high (or anywhere in between) on permissive, authoritarian, and authoritative parenting. We also measured campers' goals in basketball—e.g., did they focus on improvement (a task goal) or on winning (an ego goal)? Finally, we measured campers' intrinsic motivation and their sportspersonship (i.e., values of fair play, being a good sport, winning with grace, losing with class, respecting officials and opponents, etc.).

We found that children with authoritative parents were more likely to adopt goals in basketball in which they focused on improving their skills (task-oriented goals), but not more likely to focus on winning (ego-oriented goals). Subsequently, we found that these task-oriented goals predicted higher levels of both sportspersonship and intrinsic motivation. Thus, we found a clear pattern of results that indicate that parents who are authoritative are more likely to have children who focus on improving, and these improvement-focused children were in turn more likely to play fair, be respectful, and enjoy basketball. Although these data are correlational, and we don't know the causal direction of the findings, they do speak to the powerful connection between authoritative parenting and several positive outcomes. Once again, balance—in this case a balance of love and discipline—seems to be ideal compared to a parent who is purely permissive or authoritarian.

Conclusions on Balance

Over the past several decades, we've seen the pendulum swing toward advocating mastery goals (as opposed to performance), cooperation (as opposed to competition), and permissive parenting (as opposed to authoritative or authoritarian). Each of these solutions seems to promote either-or thinking, as opposed to a more balanced approach. This chapter has highlighted three reasons attaining balance is a challenge: more-is-better thinking; the drive to be number one; and the difficulty of quantifying balance. I also offer three research examples that demonstrate the benefits of balance.

So what does a balanced family in youth sports look like? What family could serve as a prototype for balance? Is there a family in which healthy competition, teamwork, and improvement are encouraged in a home environment that provides love and discipline? How could a family accomplish these goals while maintaining a healthy level of involvement? How could the parents of such a family avoid becoming WOSPs? The next chapter is an in-depth case study of a family that exemplifies all of these traits and more. In addition, they demonstrate these qualities in a refreshing manner that other families around the United States and beyond can relate to and model their behavior after when it comes to youth sports.

Words of Wisdom for WOSPs

1. Too much of anything, even a good thing, can be dangerous.

2. An exclusive focus on winning and being number one can obscure individual development, growth, and motivation.

3. Acknowledge that balance is a priority and have regular family meetings to assess progress. Balance may be like the moon for a ship at sea—we may never get there, but without it we will be lost.

10

The Mauer Family Story

Joe Mauer was born on April 19, 1983, the third son of Teresa and Jake Mauer Jr. The Mauers older sons Billy and Jake III were three and four years older than Joe, respectively. I have known the Mauer family for decades—first from watching Joe's mom when she was a star athlete at a local high school when I was a young child. In working on this book, I realized that the Mauers embodied many of the principles I was writing about in this project.

I wanted to know, what did Joe Mauer's parents do that was so special? So I interviewed Jake and Teresa Mauer, eager to hear their parenting secrets. I was excited to finish this book with their story as a way to tie together research on sports, motivation, and parenting. Selfishly, I also thought it would allow me to cull trade secrets from these sports-parenting experts that I could put into practice with my sons Jack and Adam.

As the Mauers and I began talking, I eagerly awaited the revelation of their big secret. It was a great conversation, time flew by, and I kept waiting. The secret never came, at least not the magical, mystical, hidden gem I was hoping for—because there is no secret. Instead, throughout the interview, I was struck by the common-sense approach they took (and take) toward parenting. Nothing they said was magic, nothing they said is impossible for any parent to do. They aren't perfect. They acknowledged things they would do differently. The beauty of their approach is that it transcends geography, race, socioeconomic status, athletic ability, and intelligence. We can all employ their savvy strategies—and while mirroring their approach may not produce the next Joe Mauer, it can produce healthy, active, happy, well-adjusted children who will become productive members of society.

Jake and Teresa Mauer

Jake and Teresa both grew up in Saint Paul, and they still live in the modest house that Jake and his brothers grew up in as children. Both were athletes, and Teresa was one of the first great female high school athletes in Minnesota history. She was a star basketball and volleyball player, and she also ran track. Teresa tired of running track and tried out for the baseball team. She ruffled some feathers with this move at inner-city Saint Paul Central High School. One day, a teammate hit her in the head with a pitch during practice, but it didn't slow her down. Later that year, at the graduation party of the same teammate, she met Jake and the rest is history. Teresa was the star of the

1976 Saint Paul Central girl's basketball state championship team—in the first year Minnesota had a state tournament for girls. She was later inducted into the Athletic Halls of Fame at both Central High School and the College of St. Catherine's, where she was a two-sport star.

On both sides of the family, Joe has a strong athletic pedigree. Joe's grandpa, Jake Sr., played some professional baseball, and his grandfather's brothers were also top-notch athletes. One of Joe's cousins was a quarterback at Nebraska (Mark), another cousin is a longtime NBA referee (Ken), and still another is a WNBA referee (Tommy). Quite simply, growing up in the Mauer household meant being immersed in a culture of athletics. Throughout the city of Saint Paul, the Mauer name was synonymous with athletics.

Though I've known the Mauers for many years, we've never had the chance to sit down and talk at length about their parenting philosophy. I spoke with Joe's parents over the course of three hours in a sit-down interview at the University of St. Thomas. I also met Joe's older brother Jake III at a local restaurant for a two-and-half-hour interview. All three of them were kind enough to share insights and stories about the Mauer family traditions, rituals, parenting styles, and children's personalities. During the interview with Jake and Teresa, I was struck by how many of the commonsense principles that guided their parenting were aligned with the psychological research on parenting practices that produce children who are happy, autonomous, seek out challenges, and are resilient in the face of failure.

Joe's parents created an environment that allowed Joe to enjoy his childhood, challenge himself, and maintain strong values. In sum, they made many different choices than Marv Marinovich and Mike Agassi, and some similar ones to Earl Woods, but on a much more moderate scale. They didn't spend thousands of dollars on Joe's development nor did they have bold visions about what they expected out of Joe. In fact, the most elegant part of the Mauers' strategy in raising their sons is that it's an approach anyone can follow.

To suggest that Joe Mauer just played sports like all the other kids his age would be patently false. Joe was indoctrinated into the sports world at a young age. By the time he was four, his parents recall him hitting balls that threatened to injure the six- and seven-year-olds he was playing against, with other parents claiming he needed to be playing with older kids for their safety.

In psychology, the nature-nurture debate has raged for decades. Without question, genetics plays a role in everything from athleticism to personality to intelligence. On the other hand, environmental factors affect individuals' behavior in profound ways. Rather than searching for a clear answer, psychologists generally agree that behavior is a function of an individual's genetic makeup, personality, and the environment.

From a young age, Joe demonstrated a passion for athletics. Part of this was his environment, part of this was Joe. According to his dad, "With our family, the boys were just around it." Joe tagged along with his older brothers, hung out with uncles and cousins, and spent considerable time with his grandfather. "We wanted them to be outside. We never bought a Nintendo. We wanted them to do something. But our yard isn't very big, so we let them throw balls around the house and just play," said Teresa. The Mauer boys grew up around sports. Both Teresa's and Jake's families were intensely passionate about athletics. As a result, some of the boys' earliest memories are of watching *Monday Night Football* games with aunts, uncles, and cousins who had come over to see the game and talk sports.

Grandpa Jake worked as a bartender, but spent every day with the boys. "When I saw Joe in the backyard, he had diapers on, and he was swinging and hitting with a bat and I said, 'Geez, we've got a left-handed hitter here!'"

The boys would spend all their time playing basketball, baseball, football, and hockey. Joe said, "If Jake and Bill went down to the park, I'd follow them there."

Jake recalls that, "I'd always pick Joe before my buddies and they'd be upset. But once they saw Joe, they knew he was special."

His dad recalls, "He hit the ball so hard, he's gotta play up in age . . . kids were getting hurt!"

From the time he was twelve years old, Grandpa Jake told people Joe would be a major-league player. As hard as it is to believe, Grandpa Jake may just have underestimated Joe's prodigious talents. At the age of 32, Joe Mauer's sports bio reads as follows:

- National High School Player of the Year—Football, 2000

- National High School Player of the Year—Baseball, 2001

- All-State at Cretin-Derham Hall High School—in football, basketball, and baseball (2000–01)

- Scholarship offers from top football colleges around the country (2000–01)

- Number one overall pick in the 2001 Major League Baseball Draft

- American League Batting Champion in 2005, 2008, and 2009

- First catcher to ever win the American League Batting Championship (2006)

- First catcher to lead the American League in batting

average, slugging, and on-base percentage (2009)—and the first player to do so since George Brett in 1980

- Gold Glove winner in 2008, 2009, and 2010

- Highest single-season batting average for a catcher (.365 in 2009)

- First catcher in MLB history to win three batting championships

- American League Most Valuable Player in 2009

- $184 million dollar contract signed in 2010

- Second-highest career batting average among all active MLB players (over a minimum of five years)

Mauer is on pace to post statistics that would mark him as one of the best, if not the best, catchers in the history of baseball. A spot in the Baseball Hall of Fame looks likely. However, Mauer has not been without adversity, suffering numerous injuries the past several years. In addition, many fans and the media have lamented that Mauer's home run numbers have not kept pace with his MVP season (even though Mauer has never been a home run hitter).

Through it all, Mauer has continued to focus on baseball, impressing those who have known him since he was young. His high school football coach, Mike Scanlan, once told me, "I thought Joe was better than Chris Weinke and Steve Walsh, two quarterbacks who won national championships in college football and both played in the NFL. I always thought he was a better football player than baseball player. As good as he is in baseball, I thought his potential in football was even greater."

More in the Mauers' Own Words

On introducing their kids to sports:

JAKE JR. We wouldn't let them have Nintendo. We wanted them to have interests that would keep them busy. We told them to "Do something, don't sit around the house." They were hardly ever indoors. With our family backgrounds, they were just around sports a lot.

TERESA. We get asked quite a bit about how we raised them. As long as they were involved in something at school, whether it was drama or the band or the newspaper, get them involved in something. If they get cut from football, make sure to get them on the yearbook staff. My mom used to say "You're only thirteen once, you're only sixteen once." I came from a family of nine and even though it would have helped to work, my mom always told us we would have our whole life to work and that we should go be kids.

One of the themes that emerged loud and clear during our conversation was the premium they placed on values such as respect and discipline. Jake was more of the disciplinarian, but Teresa had no problem keeping the boys in line. Both Jake and Teresa regularly reminded the boys that their actions reflected on themselves and their family, and bad behavior was met with swift consequences. On one van ride home from a game, the boys began fighting in the back of the car.

JAKE JR. Teresa stopped the car and made them get out and walk home while we drove.

TERESA. I told them, "Get out, I'm not driving you if you act like that." Their faces showed disbelief. I drove for a while and the three of them ran alongside the car on the sidewalk. Finally after about a mile, I stopped, they got back in the car, and they sat silently the whole way home. Joe was four, Billy was seven, and Jake was eight at the time. Instead of allowing whining or fighting, we just tried to give them consequences right away to show them what was acceptable and what was unacceptable. [Not] swearing was a big rule of ours. Billy always got caught.

JAKE JR. We were big on the dish soap on the finger and then the finger in the mouth. Billy could tell you every flavor of soap Dawn dishwashing detergent has ever made! Just yesterday we were talking to Joe, asking him about our parenting philosophy. His response? "Fear!" I told him, "There is a fine line between fear and respect, Joe," and then he got quiet.

TERESA. He was half joking. But it's true; it takes a village to raise a child. Jake's dad took care of the kids while we both worked, so the boys spent a tremendous amount of time with their Grandpa Jake. Kids know, and I think they need to hear it, that if you act up in school and you walk outside with a school uniform on and start smoking a cigarette, you are reflecting badly on your family and your friends. They need to know their actions speak volumes about who they are. I think it helps to remind them of that.

It's fun to picture a Major League All-Star teetering between fear and respect for his parents when he has a $184 million dollar contract, and it's clear the Mauers commanded the respect of their children, and still do today.

JAKE JR. You need to make them accountable for everything. There are consequences when you mess up. Praise them a little bit when they do good, and that's about it. It's pretty simple. The boys stayed out of trouble most of the time, but occasionally they messed up. One time Jake and his buddy went around the neighborhood picking up the aluminum recycling cans people had put outside for curbside pickup. They didn't think it was stealing, they just thought anyone could take the cans. I came home and my whole garage was filled with aluminum cans! I was furious! It was 11:00 p.m. and I made them take the cans and put them back in every one of those recycling bins where they found them. They ended up putting them [in] a friend's garage but I didn't find that out until years later. For the three cents a pound they got for moving those cans three times, I think they learned their lesson.

On loyalty and perseverance:

JAKE JR. For some reason, Jake wanted to play hockey one year. We knew nothing about hockey and I couldn't even stand up on skates.

TERESA. All his little buddies had been playing since they were five years old and here Jake is in third grade trying to learn how to skate. We said if he wanted to try it that was fine, but he'd only been on skates twice in his life. Our rule was if you signed up for a team or activity, you had to see it all the way through. There's no deciding after two weeks "I don't like this" and leaving.

JAKE JR. We figured he'd be on the C team, but they didn't have enough kids for the A team so they came to us and said Jake's really progressing and he can be on the A team. Well, that team cost $700, and I'm thinking, "That's a bunch of crap—you just need our money!" He ended up playing that season and went the whole year without scoring a goal and barely got his stick on the puck, and we didn't know how to teach him anything.

TERESA: He had one chance to score a goal. He was wide open in front of the net and a perfect pass came his way. He could have kicked it in the goal, but it bounced right past his stick. That was his best chance, but we just wanted him to play and there's so much more to learn from sports than shooting a basketball or a puck. You interact with kids with all different personalities and you have to learn those skills sometime.

Clearly, the Mauers supported their sons no matter which sports they chose to play. Whether it was Jake playing hockey, Joe being pressured to give up basketball by MLB scouts and college football coaches, or Billy being cut from a basketball team, Jake and Teresa always encouraged their sons to follow their passions and be true to themselves.

TERESA. I grew up in a family where my dad was very into what we did. I know he was trying to correct things, but you lose a game and then the last thing you want to do is rehash the whole thing again all the way home. I came from a family with nine kids, so I think he was just trying to communicate with us because he had worked all day—but that's what we'd talk about at the dinner table. At that point as a kid, you know you messed up and you don't want to listen. Because of my experience, I always tried to ask our boys about what they thought they did right, what they thought they could have done better, what they thought their team could have done better, rather than telling them what they should have done differently.

JAKE JR. We had people blasting us for letting Joe play football in high school. Some people in baseball told us we were nuts and we were going to ruin his career. And then the football coaches were asking why he was playing basketball. Well—everyone was asking why he was playing basketball!

TERESA. The funny thing is that to this day Joe says his senior year of basketball was the most fun year he had because he knew it was probably his last chance to play organized basketball. [Author's note to Joe: When your baseball career is over, you are welcome to resume a college basketball career at the University of St. Thomas.] In fact, he was just telling Jake and Billy to save a spot for him in their pickup basketball league when baseball is done because he can't wait to play basketball again. We just encouraged all the boys to play a different sport every season. Joe was the first one we ever let play a sport out of its regular season when we let him play traveling basketball, but even then the coach knew if there was a conflict with baseball, he would go to that. When Joe was in high school, they changed the rule about the coaches working with players during the summer. Here's poor Joe entering his sophomore year, playing summer baseball, the varsity basketball team wants him at all their practices, and the varsity football coach wants him lifting every day with the team. I think each sport teaches you something different that you can use somewhere else. I think being a quarterback helped Joe in basketball, and the anticipation you learn in basketball helps in baseball. Joe started playing basketball in first grade. He was the only white kid in a gym of thirty players.

JAKE JR. We walked in and the rap music was blaring and I asked Joe if he wanted to stay. He said, "Yeah, I want to play basketball!" So I brought him over and introduced him to the coach, Ronnie Smith. Joe got in line, made a lay-up, and all the other kids clapped. He loved basketball from then on.

The Mauers talked about always watching their kids play sports, but trying to remain as relatively distant spectators. They wanted the boys to know they loved and supported them, but they also wanted them to play because they were passionate about sports. They supported the boys and tried to create opportunities for them to succeed.

JAKE JR. It was a little tough for Billy because he was always kind of behind in sports. He was only five foot five as a freshman, grew late, and ended up six five, taller than Jake or Joe. For Bill, school was number eleven on his list of ten things to do growing up. He was only a year behind Jake, who was the typical first child, great student, and the teachers all expected Bill to be a carbon copy of Jake. Bill's social, he loves to be around people, he can sit and talk with anyone and get a rapport going, but school deadlines were a little tough on him. I always told the teachers, "He's Bill, not Jake. That's why his name is Bill." We thought sending Bill to a different high school would help get him out of Jake's shadow, but it didn't work out well. Then Bill transferred to Cretin-Derham, but his late development put him a little behind. He was the first of the boys to ever get cut from anything (basketball in his junior year). He grew a lot his senior year and they asked him to try out again, but he decided to play intramurals with his friends and work on his baseball.

TERESA. He had a lot of fun in intramurals. When it comes down to it, that's what you really want. I know our boys love playing, love competing, and love trying to get better, and I hope they aren't doing it for the accolades, especially Joe. I know he's not, because whether it's at Midway Stadium, Griggs Field, or Yankee Stadium, he always plays the same way. I guess that's the way the boys are wired.

Bill went on to play baseball at Concordia University, Saint Paul, a Division II school. He excelled there and signed with the Minnesota Twins as a free agent. His minor-league career was short-lived and he now owns a successful car dealership, Mauer Chevrolet, just outside of Saint Paul.

On sibling rivalry:

TERESA. We've always said they've been each others' worst critics but they've also been each others' biggest fans. Jake came home last week and said he got a promotion. He moved from a minor-league hitting coach to a manager. Bill and Joe were so excited for him! Even Bill, when you look at the three of them, Bill isn't in baseball anymore, he's not coaching, he's working nine to five while he's got two brothers doing what he'd obviously like to be doing, but he was so excited for Jake. I'm sure deep down he's wondering, "Why not me?"

JAKE JR. I think we taught him to be pretty competitive his whole life, and even when Bill got out of sports, he went up to Gould Chevrolet, the first real job he ever had, and he sold more Chevys in the state of Minnesota than anybody. He was the number one salesman in the state that year before purchasing his own Chevy dealership.

JAKE III. Dad always told us when we were really young that your brothers will probably be the best friends you're ever going to have. I would think, "Man, I can't stand Joe right now, the kid is on my nerves because he's following me everywhere." Then once I was ten or eleven, I started to realize just how close I was to these guys. I'd get into arguments with my buddies when we were picking teams because I'd take Bill and Joe right away before I took my buddies. It'd be the three of us on a team. Now it's like we're closer with each other than any of our buddies. It's funny how it kind of evolves. Dad was right, it all works out. Joe got asked to blow the big Viking horn at a football game and he had six field passes. He brought me and my wife and Billy and his wife. That's something that he could have called anybody for, any of his teammates or other friends in town, but he called us. Neat stuff like that, we get to experience and enjoy together.

On competitiveness:

JAKE JR. Joe was violent. We thought he had mental problems. He was ornery. He was just nuts.

TERESA. They all have a short temper but we always said Joe has a long fuse. I've really only seen him lose it three times in his life. The first time he was five and he was picking at Billy. Billy had finally had enough and whacked Joe. Joe got so angry that I was holding him back with all my strength. He was growling and shaking and I'm just holding on, wondering what I was going to do when he was fifteen!

Finally some evidence that Joe, Billy, and Jake were normal boys who fought and scrapped. Of course, their competitiveness served them well in athletics.

JAKE JR. They just hated to lose. They hated it. Joe and Bill would always cry when they were younger when they lost. Jakey would never cry. They controlled their emotions more and more as they got older. Especially in baseball, you're dealing with so much failure all the time.

TERESA. We tried to help them work through things. To get them to talk about what they could have done better, to realize they weren't perfect. We tried to keep things in perspective.

JAKE III. When Joe was little, he was real mean. He was real tough. We used to have little boxing gloves. We'd go in the backyard and box. I was four years older than Joe, so I was a lot bigger, and Billy was three years older than Joe, so poor Joe would just get pounded. He'd get so mad, he'd just keep coming at you, and coming at you. Mom was real scared to send him to kindergarten because he was that way. It worked out fine, but we all were really competitive and hated to lose.

On instilling solid values:

JAKE JR. Joe came home his first year after signing for $5 million, and I said, "Joe, it's sure nice to have you home. Now please go do the dishes!"

TERESA. He was pretty good about it.

Of course he was. The Mauer brothers have never forgotten the discipline, respect, work ethic, and loyalty Jake Jr. and Teresa taught them, which was then further cultivated through sports.

Summary

The list of Joe Mauer's accomplishments is so lengthy that it's hard to believe an athlete could do so much before the age of thirty. What's unique about Joe and the way Jake and Teresa Mauer raised him? In many ways, Joe's older brothers Jake and Billy provide the clearest answers to that question. Although Jake and Billy didn't ascend to the major leagues, both of them are well adjusted, have excellent careers, and are dedicated to their families and their communities. How did all three boys turn out so well?

The Mauers used many of the principles this book discusses. They provided authoritative parenting that balanced love and support with discipline. They challenged their children to be great, but provided unconditional love when they failed (e.g., Jake's experience playing hockey). They used the ARC to success—providing *autonomy* and choice in the boys' activities, emphasizing *relatedness* and teamwork, and helping the boys strive for *competence*. Clearly, all three boys had high levels of intrinsic motivation. Finally, the Mauers exposed their boys to a wide variety of activities, resulting in the boys being free to choose their passions and chase their dreams.

In 2011, when he suffered leg problems that kept him off the field for most of the season, Joe Mauer met the most adversity he has faced in his career. Critics questioned his toughness. For the first time, he was publicly and frequently challenged. Although he didn't respond to many of the criticisms, he came back in 2012, and was among the American League leaders in batting average. Nobody is perfect, not even Joe Mauer, and his responses to adversity—including this professional challenge—may be the strongest evidence of the beneficial parenting he experienced as a child.

None of our children will go through life without pain. In fact, it wouldn't be healthy for them if they did. Rather, we should provide them challenges, encourage them to pursue their passions, dare to be great, and get back up when they're knocked down. The Mauer family is an excellent example of how children can learn the valuable lessons of youth sports in a supportive, loving, blue-collar home where values and morals trump victories and money.

Words of Wisdom for WOSPs

1. Keep it simple. Allow kids to be kids.

2. Teach and demand respect, listening, and hard work.

3. Provide ample opportunities for children to chase their passions.

11

The Final Score

I start this final chapter with a bit of a confession. I've discussed lots of noble qualities that athletics teach us . . . but apparently the ability to finish a book isn't among them. I'm more than slightly embarrassed by how long it took to write this final chapter. Let's just say it would be measured in years, not weeks or months. The competitor in me says I failed miserably over the past five years. The more rational side of me says there's a reason this chapter took so long.

Over the past five years, I've become immersed in youth sports culture. Both of my sons went from toddlers in T-ball to full-fledged traveling basketball players (much to my chagrin). I've learned a lot watching their experiences up close—some of it good, some not so good. Moreover, I've searched high and low, near and far, looking for the panacea that will restore youth sports to its proper place in society. But it's not that easy. And that, my friends, is a major part of the answer.

In some ways, I feel as if I know less than I used to about youth sports. Should we be more organized? Less organized? More disciplined? Less disciplined? Work kids harder? Have them play more games? Have more practices? Provide more challenge? More success? More learning? A case can be made for each of these strategies, depending on the child and countless situational factors. That said, there are certain areas of youth sports about which I feel a strong degree of certitude. My hope is that this chapter will at once effectively sum up the major points of this book while stimulating more thoughts and questions as we continue to strive to provide positive experiences for our young athletes.

When I teach a class titled "Motivation and Emotion," one of the units is on hunger motivation. Most students begin the chapter eager and excited to hear what the quick-fix strategies are for weight loss. After several class sessions in which we discuss homeostasis (the concept that our bodies tell us when they're hungry, thirsty, satiated, etc.) and factors that disrupt homeostasis, students are disappointed to hear the best strategies for sustainable weight loss and a healthy life are regular exercise and a healthy, balanced diet. Our bodies are wired to provide us feedback on what they need to survive and thrive. If we listen to them, we'll be fairly well off. Much like hunger, youth sports ought to be a simple topic, yet we make it more difficult than it should be.

Research helps provide a prescription for simple and effective solutions to improving the world of youth sports. In addition, while Joe Mauer's success isn't average, his family provides a simple, sustainable, and reasonable prescription for families with children in youth sports. Their prescription includes balancing basic psychological needs and providing opportunities for autonomy, challenge, life lessons, values, communication skills, discipline, resilience, and teamwork. I've tried to boil down what we know about youth sports and how we can improve the way they're structured into three categories: What we can do at the individual/family level, what we can do at the community level, and what we can do at the societal level.

How Parents Can Promote the Positives of Youth Sports

One of the many challenges of raising children is adhering to a set of family values in the face of conflicting societal values. In this section, we discuss ways parents can work to be consistent with their own values while allowing children to socialize with their peers in positive ways. In the end, many of the decisions parents make center around their values, what their goals are for their children, and how they want to invest their time, money, and energy.

Many parents lament a lack of balance in their lives. I recently ran into the same dad I wrote about in Chapter 1—the one who shared the story with me about a friend's son having to be up at 4:30 a.m. to get to three different sporting events. I asked my friend how he was doing and he told me he had spent twelve hours on a recent Saturday at the Little League baseball field. He was coaching two of his sons' teams and watching a third. He clearly enjoys the time he's spending with his son, yet twelve hours on a Saturday in June seems excessive. How do we maintain balance in our own lives and those of our children?

My son Jack is on a Little League team and in one nine-day span, he had six games in forty-eight hours one weekend and five games in forty-eight hours the next. As much as I enjoy watching him play, at times Little League spectating feels like a second job. What are some strategies for parents and children to maintain balance in their lives, derive the intended benefits of youth sports, and have an enjoyable learning experience?

Keep in Mind the Goals of Youth Sports!

Most parents don't initially sign up their children for youth sports because they're counting on a multimillion-dollar payoff fifteen years later. Most sign up their children because they want them to be healthy, have fun, meet friends, and learn to be part of a team. Many of the frustrations surrounding youth sports have little to do with these goals. If parents and children regularly evaluate their goals, which may differ across and within families, there's a great likelihood children will benefit from youth sports.

Communicate

Too often, we lose sight of the goals of athletics because we don't verbalize these goals. Take the fifth grader who's been signed up for sports every season for the past three years and has no voice in the matter or an understanding of why he's playing sports. If his parents take time to explain some of the intended benefits—even if right now he doesn't understand why they're important—there's a better chance he'll at least understand his parents are trying to do something they believe is beneficial for him. Children should also be encouraged to communicate with their parents. This can be difficult if a child feels as if she's letting her parents down, but it's critical in terms of openness, honesty, and being true to one's self. Imagine the high school student who decides she is too stressed by her academic obligations to continue to play multiple sports. If she simply quits, or her parents become frustrated the moment she informs them she's no longer playing volleyball or basketball, there's a good chance the conversation will shut down. On the other hand, if she's able to explain her academic goals, why they're important, and how she believes playing only one sport will allow her to focus on a couple goals in a manageable way—as opposed to too many goals in an unmanageable way—odds are good her parents will understand and be supportive.

Of course, communication isn't always easy, particularly when all parties involved have invested significant amounts of time and money in sports. For that reason, parents should take the lead at an early age with children, communicating their goals for their children, the role they see sports and physical activity playing in their children's lives, and ask their children to do the same. In addition, reflecting regularly on how a season is going, how a young athlete is developing, whether or not they're having fun, ways they can be a better teammate, and lessons they're learning provide regular opportunities for young athletes to communicate their goals while providing not-so-subtle reminders to both parents and children about the diverse ways youth sports can benefit children.

Know What You're Signing up For

Too often, I hear parents complain that they "had no idea of the time commitment." Now in some cases this may be true, but in others they may not have asked the right questions before a season began. Questions such as: How many games will the team play? How many practices per week? How long is the season? How much travel is involved? Are children permitted to miss practices or games for any reason (these could range from family vacations to other opportunities to fatigue)? Will there be playoffs that could extend the season? It's important to ask each of these questions, particularly if children are playing multiple sports at the same time (e.g., summer soccer and baseball or softball), it can be difficult or even impossible to attend every event.

Not only should parents ask those questions up front, they should talk to other parents whose children have played on that team or in that league. In February, two games and two practices per week for soccer don't seem outlandish. We picture a lazy summer and adding in four one- to two-hour events doesn't seem overwhelming. Then we find out practices are thirty minutes away and two hours long, kids need to arrive one hour early for games, and the team will have tournaments over five weekends during the summer. Suddenly, each of the four evenings ends up being closer to a three-hour commitment. This can make dinner hours difficult, stress parents after a long day, and take up most of the weeknights during a summer. Multiply this by two or three children and we begin to see why many parents feel like grossly underpaid chauffeurs. Add in the weekend tournaments, rained-out games that are rescheduled, extended playoffs, and pretty soon we blink and our summer is gone, and we're not sure where it went. Of course, much of this can be avoided if parents and children ask good questions up front and are honest about the level of interest and commitment they have to a team and a sport.

Be True to Your Values

It sounds childish, but parents are susceptible to peer pressure the same way children are. Most leagues, teams, camps, and tournaments don't have marketing gurus running their advertising campaigns. Parents usually hear about teams and leagues through word of mouth from other parents. As parents we want the best for our children and when we hear about an opportunity, we jump at it, not always thinking about whether or not it's the right fit for our child and our family at this time.

Each family may have different values and goals for what they want their child to learn through youth sports. Discipline. Teamwork. Competitiveness. Travel. Tough competition. Life lessons. Sticking to these core values will help make tough decisions around youth sports seem less complicated.

Be Creative

So often, our society has added structure and organization to areas that may not require it. As adults, we need to look no further than the proliferation of health clubs and gym memberships over the past few decades. To the amazement of some, before 1980 people exercised without access to premier health clubs, but typically in less structured ways. One way isn't necessarily better than the other, but it's important that we recognize there are myriad ways to stay fit. It might mean going to the health club six days per week at 6:00 a.m., but it could also mean walking or biking to work, taking the stairs whenever possible, jogging over the lunch hour, going to a park and playing pickup basketball, or even gardening and pulling weeds.

In the same vein, children played games and sports long before organized youth sports became what they are today. Several summers ago, my boys and I created a game called Blizzard Ball. I threw them a Nerf football, a tennis ball, and a rubber ball, one at a time. The football was thrown high, the tennis ball higher, and the rubber ball as hard as I could throw it. It was nearly impossible for them to catch three in a row (I adjusted the difficulty based on their age and ability), but if they did, everyone got a Blizzard at Dairy Queen. What started with my two sons grew to three kids, then four, then eight, and then fifteen! Each night kids would amble by, we'd play Wiffle ball for a while and then inevitably we'd play Blizzard Ball until my arm was dangling and the sun had set. Most nights, nobody caught all three balls, but occasionally one would, and we would all joyously (me included) head to Dairy Queen.

What struck me as much as the kids' enthusiasm for Blizzard Ball was the reaction from adults in the neighborhood out for their evening walk. They would invariably stop and ask how we'd gotten so many kids organized. I didn't have an answer for them, other than to say we went outside and kids started showing up. They were always amazed, and most commented how it reminded them of the good old days.

Over time, Blizzard Ball has evolved into different games, and many nights we end up playing Wiffle ball. Sometimes it is just me and my two sons, other nights there are two or three other kids, and some nights we have ten or twelve kids. We vary the rules based on how many kids are there, and it's entirely informal. Some nights we play, others we don't, but what has struck me throughout is how easily parents can create "less organized" sporting opportunities that children will enjoy. Furthermore, without an umpire, they have to make their own calls. I simply told them I was done making calls because it was too easy for them to rely on me to settle their disputes.

Although the level of competition may not be as high as in organized leagues, I think backyard games such as these promote so many other positive things, including neighborhood connections, kids solving their own arguments, and kids of different ages playing together. (There are nights we have kids ranging from four to eighteen years of age.) With an open mind, parents and kids can create countless games at home that teach valuable lessons and are fun at the same time.

How Communities Can Promote the Positives of Youth Sports

At the family level, difficult choices often need to be made, but these can be done as long as families stay true to their values. If they choose to immerse their children in youth sports, not have them play at all, or choose a middle ground, at least individual families control these decisions. Communities will invariably find it more difficult than families to find consensus when it comes to the values and goals of youth sports. Interestingly, many of the improvements discussed in this section bear a resemblance to those listed in the previous one. When communities provide a voice for all and outline their goals clearly, they can effectively work to implement youth sports into their towns and cities.

Within a community, leaders of youth sports will emerge. This can be both positive and negative. Sometimes the leaders can be visionary; sometimes they can be overbearing, controlling, and rigid. What is critical is that each community have a vision for (a) what youth sports looks like when programs are done well, and (b) what outcomes youth sports will produce in its young athletes.

When done right, youth sports produce iconic images of kids

playing and laughing, exercising, striving for excellence, competing, and exhibiting good sportspersonship. Adults may be watching, but they're doing so in a relaxed way, enjoying watching kids having fun, and confident that their children are learning valuable lessons along the way. All too often, as this book's many cautionary tales demonstrate, parental overinvolvement interferes with every aspect of children's youth-sports experiences. Communities and youth leagues should have regular conversations about proper parental behavior. A set of expectations ought to be conveyed clearly to parents at the outset of each season: behavior at games and practices, whether or not it's appropriate to email or call a coach with concerns, along with the proper channels to go through with any issues or concerns. Parents should be reminded that whatever they do or say in front of their children is modeling behavior.

At games, parents should understand that the less they say the better, and what does come out of their mouths ought to be positive. I've met very few children who like to hear their parents make obscene amounts of noise, question coaches, question umpires and referees, or hurl negative statements at opponents. In addition to communicating expectations, communities can make it more difficult for parents to mess things up at games. In our interview Teresa Mauer joked that parents should run on treadmills during their kids' games. That might be a challenge to implement, but a friend of mine is attempting something similar. She plans to offer yoga classes for parents during youth baseball games. Imagine the physical and psychological benefits if parents did an hour of yoga while their children were playing. Then, after the game, instead of being frustrated by umpires' calls and stressed because they didn't get in a workout, parents would be relaxed, energized, and ready to engage with their children.

I have two other friends who were admittedly overinvolved

with their children's sports, and sometimes had trouble controlling what they were saying at games. Whether it was directed at referees, coaches, or players, they realized (after some gentle prodding), that their behavior was problematic. Each of them came up with a written statement to share with their families that outlined what was acceptable and unacceptable behavior at sporting events. In each case, the note was helpful—both for the parents with behavioral challenges and the fans sitting near them at games.

Other environmental suggestions might include designating where parents can sit at games and determining whether or not they're allowed to cheer. I know of one Little League program that has seating for parents along the baselines and in the outfield only. At youth soccer, sometimes parents are told to sit or stand only on the opposite side of the field from the teams. This is in sharp contrast to many bleachers that are located directly behind home plate where parents can be heard barking things like: Bat higher! Watch the ball! Pivot on your back foot! Get closer to the plate! All of that would be more than enough to entirely confuse a youngster who's already clearly struggling to hit a fast-moving baseball or softball! I don't know any lawyers, accountants, or teachers who would want an audience hollering at their every move. (Find the appropriate precedent! Balance the debits and credits! Make them learn faster!) So why would we expect the practice would be beneficial or enjoyable for children playing sports?

Other communities have begun to structure "informal play" nights when kids show up at the park, where they're supervised, but allowed to play with others in relatively unstructured ways. There are strengths and weaknesses to both organized and unorganized sports, and exposing children to both probably provides them more opportunities to develop a wide array of the skills parents hope they learn from sports.

In the end, a community's shared vision is critical. If people agree they want to teach kids sportspersonship, work ethic, loyalty, teamwork, and unselfishness, then these should be the guiding keywords evident in all areas of the youth program. Competition should be minimized except when it teaches valuable lessons about dealing with adversity, challenging oneself, and developing resilience.

If communities can agree that they want to provide the benefits of youth sports while minimizing travel, costs, and time away from family, while focusing on skill and character development, we'll all reap the benefits of youth sports.

How Society Can Promote the Positives of Youth Sports

At the societal level, the media plays the largest role in the growth and evolution of youth sports. Once the media began glamorizing and glorifying young athletes such as Tiger Woods, the Williams sisters, Todd Marinovich, and countless others, youth sports began to change. Subtly, the stakes seemed to rise. Parents became more focused, more intense, more driven, and more committed to producing the next stellar athlete. Of course, statistics bear out the incredibly low percentage of athletes who ascend to the professional ranks, and other statistics demonstrate a frighteningly high percentage of pro athletes who end up bankrupt within several years of the end of their career.

What do parents want in return for the time and money they invest in youth sports? I contend that WOSPs begin with the best intentions, but left unchecked, these good intentions can quickly go awry. From high school awards recognized in the local sports section to multimillion-dollar paydays, we tend to prefer instant gratification.

This manifests itself in wanting our children to make the team, play more, start, score more, receive awards, earn scholarships, and maybe even earn millions.

Of course, very few children will play college sports, much less professional sports. Thus, these understandable hopes of instant gratification often overshadow many of the real benefits of sports that will be derived much further down the road. In fact, we know from psychologist Walter Mischel's classic "marshmallow experiment" the importance of delayed gratification. Mischel presented young children (aged four to six) with the choice of eating one marshmallow immediately or waiting fifteen minutes (in the presence of the tempting marshmallow) to earn an additional marshmallow. Mischel found that children who were able to delay gratification and earn the second marshmallow showed a host of positive outcomes both in the short term and, amazingly, decades later on measures of overall well-being, education, and career success!

Measuring the Intangibles

Our world is becoming increasingly driven by quantitative data. Whether it's evaluating performance, projecting athletes' success (see Michael Lewis's 2003 book *Moneyball*), or selecting stocks, data has never been regarded with more reverence. What makes youth sports complex is that most of the desired outcomes will occur down the road, and some of them are difficult to quantify even then. Discipline, competitiveness, teamwork, and persistence are all traits that develop throughout one's life and are measured in different ways in different situations. Not only are these variables difficult to measure, but once we measure them, it's often too late to fully develop them since skills are usually honed in the early years of one's childhood and adolescence. What can society do to promote short-term outcomes that should help produce these long-term outcomes down the road?

It's understandable that children gravitate toward immediate gratification, both due to their age/developmental stage and the way humans are wired. Thus, if we can make the noble goals of youth sports more visible and pertinent to their lives, we may see children and parents alike place more emphasis on character development and less on wins and losses.

All humans have basic needs, and one of these is feeling valued. Every local newscast includes a sports segment, and most name a prep athlete of the week. Almost every newspaper contains a sports section, which often features stories and box scores on all the local high school games. Is it any surprise, then, that children tend to gravitate to sports in part because it's a way to obtain positive attention? What would happen if every night on the news top students were interviewed and the most service-oriented community members profiled? What if instead of having *Parade* All-Americans, there were *Parade* Academic All-Americans? What if instead of televising high school athletes signing a letter of intent to play for an obscure Division I school, high schools promoted students committing to attend top universities around the country to focus on academics?

Keep in mind, the goal is not to discourage children from playing sports, but rather to encourage them to play for the right reasons while excelling in school and being an excellent human being. My hunch is that if we paid more attention to these accomplishments relative to sports, more children would strive for academic excellence and aspire for greatness in their daily lives.

The Story of B. J. Viau

B. J. Viau grew up in Apple Valley, Minnesota, and we recruited him to come play at the University of St. Thomas. B. J. had an excellent high school basketball career at Eastview High School, coming within one second and the most miraculous shot I have ever seen from winning a state championship. Blake Hoffarber, who played at Hopkins High School and later starred at the University of Minnesota, sank an eighteen-foot shot from his butt at the buzzer to send the championship game into overtime, where Hopkins would win the state title. Hoffarber's shot received an ESPY from ESPN as the shot of the year.

What makes B. J.'s story so fascinating is how he has used sports as a platform to bring a community together for an excellent cause. B. J.'s mom Deb was diagnosed with Huntington's disease when he was a child. Huntington's is a genetically inherited degenerative neurological disorder that typically displays symptoms in early- to mid-adulthood with a life expectancy of approximately twenty years beyond the onset of symptoms. B. J. decided to do take action. He started a fundraiser in his community where people shot free throws to raise money to find a cure for Huntington's disease.

Fast-forward fifteen years and B. J. had created an event that inspired and brought thousands of people together and had raised half a million dollars! He used athletics and the relationships he'd formed through them as a vehicle to do good. When B. J.'s mom died in 2011, I was struck by the sheer number of people who came together to support his family, remember his mom, and share in the bond B. J. and his family helped create in their community, in their local high school, and among B. J.'s coaches and teammates at St. Thomas. As parents, what could make us prouder than watching a young man deal with adversity in a manner that demonstrated all of the traits we would hope youth sports would cultivate in our children?

Conclusion

After years of studying and researching the topic of youth sports, parents, and children's motivation, I had an aha moment recently as I was finishing this chapter. A good friend and I were talking by phone about youth sports at the end of an exhausting Sunday. As I lamented how tired I was, she said, "Aren't you the guy writing a book on youth sports and parents?"

I responded yes, I was nearly finished with the book.

"So on a Sunday you went to your older son's basketball double-header in the morning, your other son's soccer game over lunch, and back to your older son's baseball doubleheader on a cool October day—and you're telling parents how to be more moderate in their approach to youth sports?"

As my sons and I were driving home from the freezing baseball game forty-five minutes from our house, her pointed question hit me like a ton of bricks. In particular it struck me that my older son had just played four games on a Sunday when technically baseball season was over (this was an extra fall league) and basketball season hadn't started (this was a preseason warm-up).

The culture of youth sports is a powerful engine in society that drives kids to play sports year round and encourages parents to sign them up for activity after activity. I was silent for a moment, before becoming more resolved to find the right balance. I turned to my son Jack, who was still shivering from the doubleheader played in near-freezing temperatures, wind, and rain, where even with their hooded sweatshirts, the kids had looked like dancers the way they were moving on the field to stay warm. "Remind me next year not to sign you up for fall baseball."

Expecting an affirmative response, I was shocked when he quickly said, "Why not, Dad?" in a surprised and sad tone.

I told him that the cold, wind, and rain on a Sunday convinced me there were better options. When I asked him if he wanted to play fall baseball again next year, he smiled and said simply, "Yes, I do."

Just when I thought I had the answer—curtailing the amount of sports is the best approach—I was reminded again how each child is different. They have different hobbies, interests, and goals. As parents, there's no recipe for raising children perfectly, nor is there a formula for how many sports they should play or how often they should play them. At the end of the day, if they're having fun, learning lessons, and spending time exercising with their friends, the best thing we can do is to let them play.

Writing this book has coincided with another journey—watching my sons move through the ranks of youth sports. I've seen the good and the bad (along with some ugly) along the way. Most of all, though, I've enjoyed watching them have fun, smile, play, and learn valuable lessons. The vast majority of kids and parents I've encountered are great people with good intentions. I find myself convinced that there are no easy answers, and any answer we come up with ought to be fluid, because our kids and their situations are always changing.

Here are ten lessons that I hope prove valuable to you. Thanks for taking the time to think about how we can be less WOSP-like while we try to provide our children experiences that help them grow, learn, and develop.

Ten Take-Home Messages for WOSPs

1. Understand that the vast majority of children will not be pro athletes. Do not expect this in any way, shape, or form.

2. Remember that sports should be enjoyable for your children.

3. Expect your children to exercise and work hard.

4. Provide choices for your children to accomplish number three.

5. Model healthy behaviors for your children (e.g., work out, make healthy food choices).

6. Avoid controlling behavior that forces children to participate in the activities you enjoy.

7. Avoid interfering in your children's teams through interactions with coaches and/or officials.

8. Play with your kids outside of organized sports.

9. Point out lessons you hope they learn on their own and from others.

10. Enjoy the time you have with your children on the field and the court. Before you know it, they'll be adults. Life is short and you can help them play hard, have fun, and learn to be great people through the lessons available in athletics.

About the Author

Dr. John Tauer is a professor of psychology at the University of St. Thomas. Tauer's research focuses on factors that affect intrinsic motivation, a unique type of motivation marked by passion and a desire to take part in an activity for its own sake. He has been published in top social and educational psychology journals, including the *Journal of Personality and Social Psychology, the Journal of Experimental Social Psychology,* and the *Journal of Educational Psychology.*

Tauer is also one of the only tenured psychology professors in the country to coach at the college level. He was named MIAC Coach of the Year in 2013 and 2015, NABC West Region Division III Coach of the Year in 2013 and 2015, and National Division III Coach of the Year (2013) by *Basketball Times.* He has one of the highest winning percentages in all of college basketball (98-19; 84 percent) and has led UST to four consecutive MIAC titles and four NCAA appearances in four years as a head coach. He is one of the only coaches in NCAA basketball who has appeared as a player, an assistant coach, and a head coach in Final Four games.

Tauer also runs basketball camps during the summer for basketball players ranging in ages from six to seventeen. Twenty years ago, he started the camps with two weeks and twenty-five kids in each camp. Today, the camps have grown to span nine weeks of the summer, with more than 1,500 campers attending annually. (For more information, visit JohnnyTauerBasketball.com.)